Advance Praise for *Parents: Get Your Head in the Game*

Stephanie Ashland, former student, Jefferson High School, Bloomington, Minnesota. She writes: "Terri has been a guiding light for me during adolescence. She has greatly influenced my life and without her I do not believe I would have completed High School. I am now a college graduate and have enduring respect and admiration for Terri as well as hold her wisdom close to my heart."

Justine L., current student, Jefferson High School, Bloomington, Minnesota. She writes: "Ms. McCarthy offered support, understanding, and confidentiality when I was struggling with substance abuse. She has saved my life through intervention with my parents and treatment suggestions."

Vena L., parent of a Jefferson High School student, Bloomington, Minnesota. She writes: "Terri's open door as a high school chemical dependency counselor helped my daughter get pointed in the right direction to recovery. Her knowledge and experience is first hand. She understands the pain that families go through with these struggles. Thank-you for helping us."

PARENTS!
GET YOUR HEAD IN THE GAME

COACHING WINNING PARENTS · 28 Years · COACHING WINNING PARENTS

PARENTS 00 · KIDS 21

by Terri McCarthy

BEAVER'S POND PRESS

PARENTS! GET YOUR HEAD IN THE GAME © copyright 2010 by Terri McCarthy. All rights reserved. No part of this book may be reproduced in any form whatsoever, by photography or xerography or by any other means, by broadcast or transmission, by translation into any kind of language, nor by recording electronically or otherwise, without permission in writing from the author, except by a reviewer, who may quote brief passages in critical articles or reviews.

ISBN 10: 1-59298-311-1
ISBN 13: 978-1-59298-311-7

Library of Congress Catalog Number: 2009940938

Printed in the United States of America

First Printing: 2010
Second Printing: 2010

14 13 12 11 10   6 5 4 3 2

Cover and interior design by James Monroe Design, LLC.

Beaver's Pond Press
7104 Ohms Lane, Suite 101
Edina, MN 55439–2129
952-829-8818
www.BeaversPondPress.com

To order, visit www.BeaversPondBooks.com
or call 1-800-901-3480. Reseller discounts available.

To my mom, who taught me valuable life lessons, in spite of the many obstacles she faced. To my children, who inspire me to be a better person, and my husband for being a devoted hands-on dad.

Contents

Introduction . . . . *vii*

I. The Journey Begins. *1*

II. Parents' Most Common Concerns *11*

III. Sleep Issues. *29*

IV. Potty Issues. *37*

V. Eating Habits *43*

VI. Tantrums *49*

VII. Separation Anxiety. *61*

VIII.	School Performance	69
IX.	Friendship	81
X.	Puberty	91
XI.	Peer Pressure	95
XII.	Sex	101
XIII.	Drugs	115
XIV.	Internet Safety	133
XV.	No Do-Overs	139
	Index	151

Introduction

Baby Betsy is crying and by the smell of things, the reason's apparent. Timmy toddler is having a tantrum because he can't have cookies before dinner. Mary the middle-schooler is whining because she needs help with her math assignment. Math was one of your better subjects, but you can't make heads or tails out of these new fangled methods. Meanwhile, Tommy teenager waltzes in glassy-eyed and grinning from ear to ear. There is a distinct odor of sweet smoke that surrounds him, and it's not the dinner that's burning on the stove. Before you can stop him, he's chowing down the bag of cookies that you denied his little brother. Your partner of course is AWOL.

Who is this poor sucker I'm describing? It's you; it's me. It's Pat or Paula Parent at anytime from Anytown, USA. Children are like the weather; you never know what to expect. One minute it may be warm and sunny, the next minute lightning strikes. Savor those warm, sunny times, and prepare yourself for a storm.

You always have choices.
You could do one of the following:

- ✔ Run for your life.
- ✔ Call 911.
- ✔ Scream bloody murder.
- ✔ Give yourself a time out.

Let's go with the time out. Go to your room alone and shut the door, lock if necessary. Tell yourself, "I am in charge." Breathe and repeat several times. Now prioritize each calamity according to urgency. When you are confident you will not cause anyone bodily harm, return to the storm. It's time to show the family what you're made out of. Shake it off, roll up your sleeves, and breathe. It's GO time.

You choose to do the following:

- ✔ Turn off the stove, as to not burn the house down.
- ✔ Change the baby's diaper so she doesn't get a rash.
- ✔ Put Timmy in a time-out until he is done with his tirade.

INTRODUCTION

- ✔ Have Mary call a classmate that actually gets the math.

- ✔ Escort Tommy into the bathroom and have him pee in a cup.

You have provided a temporary fix to what could become a lasting solution, if you follow-up and stick with it. Now give yourself a big pat on the back. Have a good piece of chocolate or an ice-cold beer. Bask in the glow of the sunshine, and prepare yourself for the next storm to roll in.

As a school counselor for twenty-eight years, a parenting consultant, and a parent of three, I have ideas to assist you before the next storm arrives.

I
The Journey Begins

It was the best of times, it was the worst of times. Ready or not, here they come. A kid is like a box of chocolates. It doesn't get any better than this. Buckle your seat belts; you're in for a bumpy ride. What goes around comes around. The apple doesn't fall far from the tree. Don't sweat the small stuff. This too shall pass. I could've had a V8. They are my ticket to heaven, to hell, and back. Don't give up the ship. Houston, we have a problem. . . .

As a parent, you will probably experience all of these sayings and clichés—and then some. Your feelings for your children will be like no others. You will endure a range of emotions, most of them good, that you did not know existed. Your children will test you, taunt you, charm you, and revere you. They will affect you deeply—to your very core—and through it all, your love will remain constant. Your children are a part of you, something you have actually created. There is a bond between you that can never be broken, even in the bad times. That is why this venture that you are undertaking is the most important thing you'll do in your lifetime. You will be molding a child's life. It will be the toughest thing you've ever done, if you do it right. Anyone who says that parenting is a piece of cake isn't doing his or her job. That said, with parenting comes a heap of responsibility. Does that scare you? It should.

Having kids forced me to grow up. I was once a free-spirited party girl. Now, pajamas, popcorn, and SpongeBob suit me just fine. I remember telling my friends B.C. (before I had children) that I would not allow my life to change when I had children. I would continue to enjoy my social life and all of my outside interests and hobbies. I would simply include the baby. What a silly, silly, ignorant girl I was. Talk about a rude awakening! I did not consider the lack of sleep, countless diaper changes, laundry, breast-feeding, and pumping. The preparation it required just to take the baby to the grocery store was a feat in itself. It was like prepping for a journey to some distant land.

Outings had to be scheduled around nap times and mealtimes or there would be hell to pay. Planning for a simple errand with the baby in tow was mind boggling. It would go something like this: pack the diapers, the nuk, the blankie, a toy to entertain, the spit rags, the wipes, the ointment, and a bottle, of course. Wait a minute; I have to pump before we leave. I mustn't forget the breast pads in case of leakage; it's not a good look. Fold up the stroller and get it in the car. Did I even brush my teeth today, or my hair? It's all a blur. I sure hope I don't run into anyone I know. I'll grab the sunglasses and baseball cap (that's "mom chic"). Whoops, need a car seat. Just like that, in a flash (two hours) we're off. Oh crap, it's nap time. The best-laid plans. . . .

How in the world could such precious little bundles take so much time and effort? For me, this scenario was only the beginning. Diapers and bottles don't last forever, but each chapter of a child's life brings on a new challenge. I never worked so hard at anything in my life, and I can honestly say that nothing has ever brought me more pure elation. It was true: my social life took a nosedive, but I was okay with that. I was completely smitten. She had me hook, line, and sinker. She had me at hello (sorry, I couldn't resist!)

> Just like that, in a flash (two hours) we're off. Oh crap, it's naptime. The best-laid plans. . . .

There is no doubt in my mind that my children have made me a better person. Being a parent has put things in perspective for me. My children keep me grounded and thankful for my newfound life. Everything we say and do as parents from the moment of our children's births affects their lives. They are reflections of you, so you better clean up your act. No more partying into the wee hours of the night. Parenting is excruciating when you're hung over, and you can only use that twenty-four-hour flu story so many times.

You now need to censor your language. Those swear words that rolled off your tongue when you broke a nail or stubbed your toe must come to a screeching halt. If you have to say it, and sometimes we do, try to hold it until you're out of earshot, then let it fly. When it comes to a slip of the tongue, I swear my kids have radar. They may not hear anything I say but if I let a profanity slip, they are all over that. They imitate your actions and your words. You do not want to get a report from school saying your child called his teacher a dumb ass. This is your time to shine. Roll up your sleeves, step up to the plate, and get ready to play ball. It's crunch time. Remember: the apple DOESN'T fall far from the tree.

> You don't want to get a note from school saying your child called his teacher a dumb-ass.

Read books, talk to your doctor, and consult other professionals, parents, relatives, and friends. Each source will share something worthwhile. Keep in mind that your intellect will often be clouded by your undying love. You may be so enamored by the very thought of your child that clear thinking becomes a thing of the past. You may have great intentions, but the slightest sign of distress from your child may dissolve intelligent, objective thinking. GET A GRIP; don't succumb to tears or "Daddy, please!" or "All of my friends are allowed." If you do, the miracle you created could turn into a monster.

Establishing good, sound, practical rules early on will help you deal more easily with their later childhood years. There's a simple reason for this; they'll know what to expect from you. Keep in mind that there are countless variables that enter the parenting picture. Here are a few:

- ✔ The way you were parented
- ✔ Your life experiences and values
- ✔ Your education
- ✔ The number of children you have
- ✔ Whether you work inside or outside of the home
- ✔ Whether you parent alone or with another person
- ✔ Your age when you have children

Where do you start? With a loving, grateful heart and fingers crossed. Focus on and recognize positive behaviors. Don't sweat the small stuff, or you'll drive yourself crazy. Life is short, so pick your battles wisely. Use trial and error, and learn from mistakes as you go along. Maintain a sense of humor. Be open-minded and willing to go back to the drawing board to change the game plan when necessary. An intervention that worked one month may not work the next. An intervention that worked with one child may not work with the next.

And try to stay one step ahead. Always keep your children's best interests and your sanity in mind. Attending to their best interests does not mean catering to their every whim or that you allow them to run the show. If you do, they will suck the life out of you. Tell yourself, "I AM IN CHARGE." Breathe and repeat. Make this your mantra.

Children need boundaries. Without them, they feel insecure and unloved. Their world will not end if you say no. They will not hate you forever. They will not die if they don't get the gummy bears they want in the grocery store or if you say no to *Freddie Krueger XI*. They need to hear no sometimes so that they can learn to deal with disappointment. That short word "no" can become your friend. Let's say your child asks you to do something for him that you know he can do on his own, like tie his shoes. He'll put on that sad little puppy-dog face and say "Pwease, Mommy!" DON'T FALL FOR IT; get a hold of yourself. It may take him longer than it would take you, but he'll never get it if you keep doing it for him. Just picture in your mind tying your son's size fifteen shoes on prom night. Is that what you want? I think not.

Allowing them to help themselves leads to self-reliance and a sense of accomplishment. Give children the opportunity to work some things out on their own, to do things for themselves. This fosters learning, independence, and self-esteem. These are feelings that can't come from you.

I worked with a sixteen-year-old who was very depressed and so desperate to feel better that he flat out asked his parents for rules and boundaries. This was a first for me in my twenty-eight years of working with children and families. I've had students hint at this, but they usually back peddle before the conversations were over. I will call this young man Mark. Mark was experiencing severe depression and had been self-medicating with drugs. This, of course, wasn't working for him. He managed to mask his feelings when he was high, but when the high wore off, he felt worse than before. (I will address this kind of scenario in more detail in chapter XIII.) He was failing all of his classes. His parents were too busy and preoccupied with their own issues to really know what was going on with Mark. They did not see the elephant in the room. This sometimes is a defense mechanism with parents, because drug use is often more than they can handle.

> His parents did not see the elephant in the room

Mark was sent to the office because—once again—he was sleeping in class. Sleeping was another escape for him, something he needed because he wasn't capable of handling reality. The principal gave him a pep talk/warning about this behavior, and he came directly to my office after speaking with her. He told me what had happened, put his head in his hands, and cried. It was obvious to me that what was making him cry wasn't this incident, but his life in general. He was caught in a cycle: depression, using, and back to depression. So what came first, the chicken or the egg? It no longer mattered. What we knew for sure was that his life had spiraled out of control and he was desperate for help.

The following needs emerged from our discussion, at his request:

1. I need rules at home.

2. I need a curfew.

3. I need my parents to check up on me when I go out.

4. I need my parents to check on my schoolwork.

5. I need them to drug test me, and maybe get me in to treatment.

6. I need counseling, and maybe medication.

Mind you, I did not coach him in any way. These were his words. He hadn't discussed any of this with his parents, because they had their own problems and he didn't want to be a burden to them. We decided to bring in his parents as soon as possible to discuss his needs. We needed to strike while the iron was hot. I did not want to take the risk of Mark backing out.

His mom was unable to come in until the following day. When she came in, however, Mark stood firm about his needs. His mom was very receptive and willing to do whatever it would take to help him. She had no idea that he was so miserable. She thought she was doing him a favor by allowing him the freedom to make his own choices. His take was this: they were too busy, too concerned with their own problems, and just didn't care.

Communication in the family had ceased to exist. This could very well have been the source of Mark's problems. I was hopeful that this meeting had opened the door to more effective family communication. We developed a step-by-step plan to dig Mark out of his deep hole of disparity. I drew up a contract that addressed his specific needs. (See chapter XI for a sample contract.) I encouraged Mark and his parents to enlist the entire family in this mission. The contract included the following tasks:

- ✔ Make an appointment with a chemical health counselor.
- ✔ Make an appointment for a psychological evaluation.
- ✔ Check schoolwork daily.
- ✔ Know where he's going and with whom.
- ✔ Enforce a curfew.
- ✔ Give random drug tests regularly.
- ✔ Be consistent and following through to help Mark to succeed.

Mark's story is a concrete example of why children need clear boundaries. Always saying yes may be easy, but it can give a child a sense of entitlement. This carries over to other aspects of their lives, including relationships, success in school, and, quite frankly, all other endeavors. They will learn to become dependent on others and will have little confidence in themselves. If the enabling parent isn't there to help or bail the child out, she will most likely fail or quit. Such a child will not put her best foot forward or persevere when times are tough, because she will expect to be rescued. This will lead to failure and a whole slew of disappointments in life. Do you want your child living with you forever? I didn't think so.

> They are not capable of making decisions in their best interest, that's why they're called CHILDREN.

You need to establish rules for yourself before you can discuss your children's boundaries with them. What might those rules look like? Do not pick up the baby every time he cries. Do not give in to tantrums. Do not allow the kids free range to choose their food, their TV shows, their bedtimes, where they sleep, etc. They are not capable of making decisions that are in their best interests; that's why they're called CHILDREN. Use good common sense. Maintain a sense of humor, and remember, YOU ARE IN CHARGE. Breathe and repeat.

II
Parents' Most Common Concerns

The following list includes what parents have reported to me, over the course of twenty-eight years in education, to be the most difficult issues they face:

1. Sleeping issues
2. Potty issues
3. Eating issues
4. Tantrums
5. Separation anxiety
6. School performance
7. Friendship problems
8. Puberty, moods, and defiance

9. Peer pressure

10. Sex

11. Drugs

12. Internet dangers

A good way to start addressing these problems is to discuss parenting ideas with your partner. Find a middle ground you can both live with. Support one another in this venture, and don't undermine one another. If you and your partner do not agree on a rule, discuss this privately. You may need to compromise or offer a convincing argument for your ruling. When you've settled on a decision, stick to it and present it as a united front. Be careful of succumbing to the "Mom says no so I'll go to Dad the push over," tactic. When this works for kids, they may get what they want, but it creates serious problems with your credibility and their respect for you both, not to mention your relationship with your partner.

Be CONSISTENT, and FOLLOW THROUGH. Do not threaten something on which you know you will not follow through. "You're grounded for life," or "I'll kick your butt" are probably out. How many times have you said or have heard another parent say, "If you do that one more time. . ."? The "one more time" usually becomes five or ten more times. When you say things like this and don't follow through, your children lose trust in you.

If you're too angry for rational thinking or decisions,

WALK AWAY. Take as much time as you need. Sometimes you may need to give yourself a time-out. When you can speak clear English and the vein in your forehead no longer bulges, proceed with caution. Here are some ideas you may find helpful:

> When you can speak clear English and that vein is no longer bulging from your forehead, proceed with caution.

- ✔ Rules should be easy to understand, simple, and to the point.

- ✔ Be REALISTIC. For example, NEVER allowing your child to have sweets will only make him want sweets more. Use common sense.

- ✔ Emphasize the positive. When you observe your children doing something well, don't just think about how pleased you are; let them know. Don't hesitate to praise when others are present. These bystanders may also recognize or praise our child, reinforcing the desired behavior.

- ✔ Reprimand privately. There is no reason to share your disappointment or anger with your child in the presence of others. Why? First, it is no one else's business. Second, your rules and consequences may differ from those of others. Adding embarrassment to an already bad situation is redundant and potentially harmful. Children do not learn lessons from this kind of attention, only hurt and resentment. Reprimanding publicly may also make other people who are present uncomfortable.

✔ Criticize the choice, not the child. For example, compare "Hitting your sister was a bad choice" to "Only a bad kid would hit her sister." If you respond with the second kind of statement often, the child will believe she is a bad person and will behave accordingly.

✔ Be actively involved in their lives. This shows your children that you are interested and that you care.

✔ Keep the lines of communication open. Initiate conversations. Instead of using open-ended questions such as, "How was your day?" (to which they will most likely respond, "Fine," or "Boring!") be specific and say something like, "Tell me what you did in art class today."

✔ Be approachable and listen. Actively listen to what your child says. Repeat in your own words and respond. If the news is bad, try not to overreact. Appreciate the fact that your child came to you with the truth. This may result in a consequence, but let him know that it would have been much worse had he not been honest.

✔ Establish routines. Children are more secure and self-confident if they know what to expect. Establish mealtimes, homework times, curfews, and bedtimes. With busy families, this doesn't always go as planned. You may need to make occasional exceptions, but do your best to make and follow routines the majority of the time.

✔ Compromise when possible. As mentioned in the previous point, sometimes you need to make exceptions to the rule. Maybe your rules about the amount of allowable sweets don't have to be enforced on birthdays or holidays. Maybe a curfew can be extended on special occasions, such as proms or out-of-town sporting events.

✔ Sometimes, agree to disagree. It's okay, even healthy, for your child to have a different opinion or feeling about something than you have. Allow your child the opportunity to express this. You are both entitled to your feelings.

✔ Make mistakes teachable moments. We can learn from a mistake by reflecting and exploring what might have been a better choice. Discuss how your child might have avoided the mistake, and think together before making a decision about what would have been the better, or the best, choice. What might be the consequences of the different options you are now considering? Are the possible consequences worth the risks involved? Brainstorm or even role-play about what might have been a better choice so the child has some new tools the next time he finds himself in a similar situation.

- ✔ Punishments should fit the crimes. Try to make the consequence logical. If your teen got a speeding ticket, for example, you could take away car privileges for a set amount of time. It would not make sense to force your teen to quit an extracurricular activity. The two are not connected. If your child's grades are slipping, you might establish less free time and more study time. Taking snacks away would make no sense.

- ✔ Practice what you preach. If you expect your child to mind their manners at mealtimes, then you should do the same. I have witnessed some adults model the following disgusting behaviors at mealtime: talking with food in their mouths, putting elbows on the table, smacking their lips, and using fingers for food that wasn't finger food. We were at an outing once and a dad admonished his son for smacking his lips. The son replied, "Dad, you smack all the time." His dad replied, "When you pay the bills, you can smack your lips all you want." What? This of course makes absolutely no sense. So what did the son learn? Once you're working you are entitled to be rude? Is being rude something you earn? Is being rude a reward? The son will follow orders because he has to, but will he respect his dad? Will he learn this behavior from him? Probably. Kids can also learn, however, from their parents' mistakes.

> When you pay the bills, you can smack your lips all you want.

It is a sad state of affairs when parents are poor role models, but it happens. I have worked with many children who have come from abusive homes. Unfortunately, many of them learn abusive behaviors by living with abusive parents, but it doesn't have to be that way. As parents, you may have come from less-than-desirable homes, which is very unfortunate. This does not mean that you are doomed, nor are your children. It takes extra effort and awareness to make your life and the lives of your children better than your life growing up. Righting the wrongs you've experienced might happen through therapy, education, or research, but you can do this. You can break the cycle. You can make it your mission in life not to make the same mistakes your parents did.

Please understand that I am not referring to the little imperfections we all have. I am referring to emotional or physical abuse, neglecting your child, or exposing your child to an addiction or illegal activity. From a parent, these behaviors are unacceptable.

I grew up with an abusive, alcoholic stepfather. He made my family members' lives a living hell. I honestly didn't know at the time if my family life was normal; it was all I knew.

I do believe that our family pioneered "dysfunction." We grew up in a small town in the 1960s. My mom divorced and remarried a crazy alcoholic. I did not know another family at that time in our situation. Sometimes we were called names, and there were some children that were not permitted to play with us. Humor helped us to cope. We laughed every chance we got. We put the fun in dysfunction. However, I vowed years before I had children, that if I was to ever become a mom, my children would never live that kind of life. I guess I was one of those resilient kids.

> We put the fun in dysfunction

I met with a student who is the epitome of resiliency. It was our first meeting, so I was gathering his family history. What he shared was nothing less than remarkable. He had been tossed from parent to parent, depending who was incarcerated at the time, since he was born. When he was "with" his dad, he spent more time with his father's girlfriends than his father, since Dad disappeared for weeks at a time. Whenever Mom got out of jail, she wanted him back, because he was her welfare ticket. She spent the welfare money on crack, so they frequently moved from one shelter to another.

The most recent shelter landed him at our school. Shortly after his arrival, we hooked him up with community mental health services. Now a mentor/counselor visits him at school twice a week. They made a connection. His mentor has exposed him to career training and employment opportunities. His mom, of course, moved again, out of our school boundaries. Because of the connections he had made at our school, he asked to stay. The administration agreed, but only as long as he came to school regularly and passed his classes. He actually gets up at 4:30 a.m. and catches three buses so he can attend our school, continue his education, and get the support he needs to succeed.

His story left me speechless. My response was, "Don't look back; keep doing what you're doing. Don't lose sight of your future. Be successful, not because of your parents, but in spite of them."

For parents who had this kind of experience when they were young, the first step is to recognize that it was NOT OKAY and it is NOT acceptable. The next step is to do what you have to do to heal and move past this. If you have not dealt with your own abuse as a child, you may be unwittingly passing it on to your children. You need to make a conscious effort to avoid repeating this behavior. You can be a wonderful parent if you recognize your needs and get help.

Do Not:

- ✔ Belittle, name call, or ridicule. That is what children do. You need to keep your adult cap on as a parent and resist the urge to engage in such immature behaviors. This hurts a child to her core, and kids do not forget it. If done on a regular basis, it can destroy a child's self-worth and negatively affect other aspects of her life.

- ✔ Argue with your child. When you allow this to happen, you automatically lower your parenting status to your child's level. This gives your child the power to question your authority and decisions. Allowing your child to voice his opinion is fair. The conversation should end, however, if anyone's voice gets raised or someone uses profanity. If the topic is about a no-tolerance policy you have, you may offer one explanation of that policy. Giving more than that is not necessary. End the discussion and go about your business.

- ✔ Compare siblings. This does not benefit anyone if it's done in a negative way. I will share an example that illustrates how harmful this can be in chapter VIII.

- ✔ Yell or scream. Remember, you are the adult. Screaming causes fear and disrespect. Communication ceases when yelling and screaming enter the picture. Children will also emulate this behavior with others, which will cause social and behavioral problems for them.

- ✔ Use corporal punishment. Children do not learn lessons from this, only fear, anger, and resentment.

According to studies done by Murray Straus and Denise Donnelly, spankings and other forms of corporal punishment are most likely to backfire. Murray Straus, a professor of sociology at the University of New Hampshire and co-director of the family research laboratory at UNH, is the author of *Beating the Devil Out of Them*. Donnelly is a professor of sociology at Georgia State University. She studied with Straus at UNH and co-authored his book. They maintain that although the intention of corporal punishment is usually to stop a child from misbehaving, it actually leads to more serious problems in the future. Hitting and spanking can lead to impaired learning and delinquency. Later in life, children who have endured corporal punishments from their parents may become violent, depressed, and turn to criminal behavior.

Dr. Larzelene, associate professor at the University of Nebraska Medical Center, offers an opposing view, however. He has studied spankings for twenty-five years and states that non-abusive spankings are a safe and effective form of discipline for preschool-age children. He points out, however, that spanking only works when parents act calmly. Angry spankings happen when parents spank on impulse; these are harmful. He also notes that these parents report feeling remorseful afterwards. So angry spankings don't just hurt the child.

> If parents allow themselves "cool down" time before they spank, will they still choose to spank?

Here's some food for thought. If parents allow themselves "cool down" time before they spank, will they still choose to spank?

And here are a few other helpful hints:

✔ Treat children with respect; they are human beings and they deserve this. Try to imagine yelling and shaking your finger at a co-worker because she forgot to return the stapler she borrowed. Sound ridiculous? Then why is this behavior okay with a child? "Please return the stapler when you're done" should work in both situations.

- ✔ Admit when you make a mistake and learn from it. Kids love this; it makes you human. Being a parent doesn't mean you know everything or that you're perfect. If you messed up, suck it up and admit it. Discuss what you should have done differently and what you'll do in the future. And by all means, apologize when you should.

- ✔ If you do not have the answers, admit it and try to find them. Sometimes we need to turn to someone with more experience or expertise. This is healthy; you can learn together as a family.

- ✔ Model positive interactions with your partner, friends, and family members. The best way to teach your children how to get along with others is to model those behaviors. They watch and copy the good and the bad.

- ✔ Get to know your children's friends and their friends' parents. This gives you great insight into your child's personality, interests, and behaviors. If your child's behaviors suddenly change, either for the good or bad, chances are that her friends are influencing them. If it's for the good, encourage and reinforce. If it's a problem, don't waste any time getting to the bottom of it.

- ✔ Always rule out physical problems first. If your child is going through a difficult time, whether academic, emotional, or social, a physical problem could be at the root of it.

- ✔ Address mental health issues, and seek professional help if necessary. If problems persist with no obvious explanation, ask your physician for a referral to a mental health professional. This does NOT mean anyone is crazy. A chemical or hormonal imbalance can throw off anyone's psyche. There are many remedies available for these issues, including talk therapy, exercise, journaling, art, music, medication, and behavior modification.

Communication Basics

You can begin teaching your children basic communication at a very early age. At the age of two or three, children can identify some of their fundamental feelings. This is where you start. When your child is upset or having a hard time expressing himself, ask him if he can tell you how he feels. Chances are, he'll say, "Bad." You can help him identify that feeling by adding, "Is it a sad bad, a scared bad, or an angry bad?" You could take it a step further by showing him an expressions feelings chart. A wonderful feelings face poster is available online at www.childtherapytoys.com. I use this often when working with elementary students. This poster displays every feeling imaginable. Your child is sure to find and express the way he is feeling. It's also fun, because the faces are cartoon-like. Being able to identify and share a feeling helps relieve some of the stress of experiencing that feeling.

The second step is to find out why your child feels that way. Determining the cause with a very direct question is best. For example, you might ask, "What happened to make you feel scared?"

The third step is to figure out what to do to help your child feel better. Again, asking a direct question is best when communicating with small children. So you might ask, "What could you do to feel better?" Have your child brainstorm ideas. Help him decide what would work best for him.

It is important to give your child ownership of the feeling, the reason for the feeling, and the solution. Listen to what he has to say, and reflect on his statements to help him understand and remember. If you model this basic communication and your child practices it, it eventually becomes a learned behavior.

These basic principles always apply and will be helpful when communicating with your child. Just keep in mind that as children mature, the basics become more sophisticated.

Basic Communication Principals:

- ✔ Have your child share his feeling, using an "I" statement.

- ✔ Have your child share the reason he feels that way.

- ✔ Have your child share a request about what might make him feel better.

It may go something like this for your child: "I feel scared because I had a bad dream. Could you tuck me in and tell me a story?"

It's important that children know that they may not get exactly what they want to help them feel better. Going to Disney World is a great idea, but not always a very practical one. If you help children brainstorm, together you'll discover reasonable solutions. As I mentioned, just expressing their feelings gives children a sense of relief.

It is also helpful to consider the following when communicating your feelings with your children. Whenever possible, communicate face-to-face. Given the electronic era we now find ourselves in, too often we settle for an e-mail, text, or phone call. These tools are certainly convenient, but they should never entirely replace face-to-face communication, especially when the topic is important. Communication is more than talking. There is listening, of course. Tone of voice is also very telling. The exact same verbiage can be delivered many ways to mean different things. An e-mail, text, Facebook comment, etc. certainly cannot pick up on that. A phone conversation might, but then you're missing facial expressions and body language. It's tough to get a sense of these subtleties if the other person is not present. If you want the whole enchilada, communication is best accomplished when you are face-to-face, better yet, one-to-one—with few or no distractions. An audience may stifle or exaggerate your true feelings. This also means no cell phones, headphones, TV, or computer during the discussion.

Let's recap the key ingredients of great communication. They include the following:

1. Face-to-face discussion
2. One-to-one interaction, with no audience
3. Your child using "I" statements
4. Your child sharing his feeling(s)
5. Your child sharing the reasons he feels as he does
6. You and your child sharing desired outcomes

As I mentioned, this does not guarantee that you'll get exactly what you want, but your message will be very clear.

III
Sleep Issues

I will probably make this statement before I address every issue: rule out any physical problems before tackling important issues. If your doctor gives your child a clean bill of health, you can now get to work on conquering sleep issues.

These can be anything from your baby not sleeping through the night to your child having nightmares.

Let's start with what we've all experienced: baby not sleeping through the night.

If you have heard parents brag that their child slept through the night as soon as they brought the little bundle home from the hospital, they were delirious from sleep deprivation. When it comes to an infant's sleep patterns, parents should start out with low expectations.

It will probably be weeks, maybe months, before the monumental moment occurs: baby sleeps sweetly and soundly without waking for eight full hours.

Because the sudden lack of sleep can be difficult for new parents, having both parents at home or another family member to help out the first few weeks is a must. The adjustment is particularly difficult for Mom and baby. They both need sleep. If Mom is going it alone from the get go, she will not have the energy or brainpower to focus on the baby's sleep schedule. With help, you can begin implementing sleep strategies from the day the little bundle arrives.

> Do not rush to rescue the little critter every time it cries.

Do not rush in to rescue the little critter every time it makes a noise, whether it's a burp, gurgle, or squawk. If the child cries, give her a few minutes until you pick her up. Babies usually cry for a reason. They may be wet, hungry, or gassy—probably all of the above. Clean and change her, and make sure she is thoroughly dry.

Feed her. The amount will depend on her size and the time of her last feeding. Keep her awake during this time to make sure she eats her fill. A baby's digestive system is very small the first three to four months. This means your child will need to be fed often, every three to four hours. After you feed her, always attempt a burp; she most likely will have an air bubble anxious to reach the surface.

SLEEP ISSUES

Swaddle, snuggle, and soothe her until you can feel she is relaxed, even if she is not necessarily sleeping. To do this you can rock her or sing or talk softly to her. What else can relax your baby? Babies find sucking soothing. Most doctors agree that giving an infant a pacifier is okay. The baby should be at least six weeks before you introduce a pacifier and you should take it away when the baby's around a year old. Babies are also used to the sound of swishing in Mom's uterus. Some parents find white noise helpful. Finally, lay your baby down on her back with the head of her bed slightly elevated. If she cries, softly caress her, but do not pick her up. Then leave the room.

Children will learn very quickly when you answer every whimper. They will whimper a lot. Why not? This behavior gets them what they want: you at their beck and call. So instead of crying for their true, basic needs, the child will cry to manipulate. Yes, I said manipulate. And I mean manipulate you. It's Pavlov's theory of stimulus and response, and it's innate in humans and animals. The stimulus is their crying; the response (pay-off) is your rushing to their rescue.

> The stimulus is their crying; the pay-off (response) is your rushing to rescue them.

Try this: Pick up your infant when he cries (after you meet all of his basic needs). If he immediately stops, he really didn't need anything. Put him back down. If he instantly begins to cry again, he is training you. Why should he stop, if that's what gets him what he wants? By continuing to pick him up whenever he cries, you give your baby the message that whenever he wants something, all he has to do is cry. This expectation will carry over into toddlerhood, your child's preschool years, his later childhood, and eventually his adulthood. This is often in the form of whining and complaining. You have created a manipulator, and he has created a wimp.

When you know that you have met all of your child's needs after your child cries, you can experiment a little. If she cries a short time later, time it. The first time she starts, let her cry between five and ten minutes before you check on and soothe her. The next time, wait fifteen to twenty minutes, and every time she starts again, increase the time you wait by ten more minutes. This will seem like hours, but hang in there; be tough. Your baby will eventually realize that her crying will get her nothing but tired. When she is due to be fed, make sure you check on her or answer her cry. If you stick to this, the too-frequent waking should subside in a matter of days.

As we noted, a pacifier may be of assistance to help calm and soothe a crying baby. According to the Mayo Clinic Foundation for Medical Care and Research, providing a pacifier is actually a better option than letting your child suck his thumb. If he's already eaten and has had his fill but is still fussy, a pacifier may do the trick. Pacifiers are especially handy when the baby fusses in public.

You should have more than one on hand so that you can always offer your baby a clean one, wherever you are. Make sure to discard any broken pacifier to avoid bacteria getting trapped inside or the possibility of your baby choking. You can wean your baby from the pacifier around the same time you introduce him to a cup. At around twelve to eighteen months, a child's need for sucking is less noticeable. A special toy or stuffed animal may now suffice to calm him.

Please note: During the day, it's a good idea to try to keep the baby awake some of the time. This is a great time to cuddle and coo. Putting your child in a baby chair and having him keep you company as you go about your daily routine is also good for both you and your baby.

Nightmares

Nightmares are something we all experience at times. They are haunting, nagging nighttime sleep invaders. Many theories speculate about why we have them. It may be because we're experiencing stress in our lives or have unfinished business. We might be internalizing something that reveals itself in a dream. Interrupted sleep may bring on a bad dream. A nightmare may be due to an illness that causes a fever. The cause could also be as simple as something we ate that did not agree with us.

As adults, we can wake up from a bad dream and realize it was just that. Children have a more difficult time differentiating dreams from reality. When children wake up from bad dreams, what they know at that moment is fear. It is our job as parents to offer calm, comforting, and rational responses. A cold drink of water, a favorite stuffed animal, or short story also helps to distract them.

Sometimes just being held and rocked is enough for a small child. It's best to try to keep children who have woken at night in their own rooms, in their own beds. It is very tempting to take a scared child into your own bed, but once this starts, it's tough to stop. But again, there are always exceptions to the rule. If everyone is losing sleep because of your child's nightmares or wakefulness, you may need to bring her into your room on occasion. If you think it is best for your child to sleep in the room with you under special circumstances, you can make up a bed for her on the floor so that your sleep is not interrupted. But with an older child, a simple explanation about dreams—that they are not real—may be enough to keep her in her own bed.

> Make bedtime a pleasant, soothing, relaxing time, so the child goes to bed feeling stress free.

You can do a few things to help prevent those pesky nightmares. Bedtime should be routine. Try to stick to a similar pattern every evening. Make this a pleasant, soothing, relaxing time, so your child goes to bed feeling stress free. Most children enjoy a snack before bed. Try to make it something light and easy to digest, such as crackers, pretzels, or a banana. Avoid sweets, anything with caffeine, and heavy, greasy foods. A warm bath is very relaxing. After tucking your child in, end the day peacefully with a short story or prayer, or by recounting what you are thankful for.

Do not allow children to watch anything violent or scary if they are under twelve, especially before bed. Make sure they have time to wind down at least an hour before bed so they can begin to relax. Try to avoid conflict or any excitement before bedtime. Although these are not foolproof methods, they certainly can help.

"Night terrors" are a different ball of wax. Dr. Vincent Ianelli studies these phenomena. He is a pediatrician in Dallas, Texas, and also an associate professor at the University of Texas SW Medical School in Dallas. He explains that night terrors occur during deep sleep. During night terrors, children are aroused and usually yelling or screaming and standing or sitting bolt upright. They are inconsolable and very difficult to wake; waking them may take a few to several minutes. Night terrors are usually infrequent and subside by adolescence. And they are definitely scarier for the parents, because the child is unaware of what's happening and will have little or no memory of it in the morning.

There is no definitive answer about what causes night terrors. Sleep studies have discovered, however, that they happen most often to children under the following circumstances: stress, medication that affects the brain, being overtired, or eating a heavy meal before bedtime. Eliminating some of these causes may put an end to these troubling nighttime events.

When I was eight or nine, my mom gave my older brother and sisters permission to see a scary movie at a theater. I was highly insulted that I was not allowed to go along. It wasn't so much that I wanted to see the movie, but not to be included with the rest of the group really rubbed me the wrong way. My mom felt (rightly so) that I was too immature to handle a movie about an ax murderer. She knew that I was a chicken little and that seeing this would affect me differently than it would my siblings. I begged and pleaded as I had never done before. My siblings even chimed in, saying it wouldn't be so bad. She finally gave in—she rarely did that. Boy, was that a mistake.

I was so scared at the theater that I literally crouched under my seat and cried. I slept with my two sisters in their double bed for months. This irritated the hell out of them, but neither was willing to sleep alone in my single bed. I eventually went back to my own bed, but slept with the covers over my head for what seemed like forever. You know your children better than anyone, if you feel something is not right for them, it probably isn't. "If it looks like a duck . . ."

IV
Potty Issues

Hands down, potty training is one of the least fun experiences for parents. No matter what the experts say, there is no patent on potty training. There is no magic technique or time for this milestone. What worked for my mom may not work for me. What worked for one child, may not work for another. My husband was so frustrated at one point with our almost-three-year-old who showed no interest in using the potty that he offered her $500.00. That worked like a charm—NOT. Did she understand what she was supposed to do? Absolutely. She simply had no interest. It was an inconvenience, interrupting playtime, snack time, and other pleasant activities. After all, she had the convenience of the port-o-potty strapped to her rear-end.

How do you know when it's time, and where do you begin? This is no scientific method. It's trial and error involving Pavlov's theory of stimulus and response. In other words, it's all about behavior modification, or recognizing and rewarding positive behavior.

So when do you start? When they start toddling, allow them to accompany you to the bathroom so they can observe how it's done. You don't have to do this every time. You are entitled to a little privacy. Whenever possible, have your boy accompany Dad or an older male sibling and your girl accompany mom or an older female sibling. Of course, boys can certainly start by sitting on the toilet, so that could also be modeled by mom.

> The timing of potty training is not an exact science.

Having a small potty in your bathroom at the beginning of your child's training is a good idea. Let your child sit on it with clothes on to get the feel for it. This will assure her that there is nothing threatening about it. Now she is not just observing, but mimicking. Let her know that you are pleased she is sitting on the potty. Make the potty something special; your child's very own. You might want to put her name on it, along with some fun décor. This is what I call "the dry run."

When should you take it to the next level? In other words, when do the pants come down? Your child may already be doing this in imitation of your behavior. If not, don't force it until it's time. Take advantage of

POTTY ISSUES

opportunities when she's already bottomless; after a diaper change or a bath are perfect opportunities. Now, step up the motivation by offering a reward just for sitting her bare butt on the potty. Some immediate reward is great, like a sticker or a small treat (maybe a few M&M's). I normally do not believe in rewarding with food, but small amounts in this case may be acceptable. Have the stickers or treats in plain view so she'll be reminded of the reward (the stimulus) and associate it with the potty (the response).

Notice that I did not mention an age. That's because the timing of potty training is not an exact science. Most children cannot begin to grasp this concept before the age of two. Boys tend to take to it a little later than girls. The following are observable behaviors that may signal that they are ready:

1. Your child understands basic concepts, i.e., what happens when you're on the potty.

2. Your child can follow one- or two-part directions, such as "Please pick up your toy and put it in the toy box." If she understands this, then intellectually she may be ready to understand the idea of using the potty. By the way, it is a great idea to use a small reward for this type of behavior. Kids will quickly realize that doing things for themselves pays off.

3. Your child expresses discomfort or disappointment when he soils his diaper.

4. Your child goes off alone or out of sight to wet or soil. This indicates that she recognizes her urge to go, but possibly does not want to be inconvenienced by going on the potty. My son was guilty of this. Whenever Dan was MIA, we knew what he was up to.

Any or all of above indicate it is time for big-girl or big-boy underpants. Take your child shopping with you, and allow him to help you pick them out. You might want to consider ones with printed action figures or princesses. A mom once shared with me that her toddler chose Spider-Man underwear because Spider-Man was his hero. She mentioned to him that his hero might not like being soiled. He was very considerate of Spider-Man and did his best not to soil him. Mom then emphasized what a considerate boy he was and the training went quite smoothly. Spider-Man took an occasional hit, but he cleaned up very nicely.

You can expect a lot of accidents and changes at first, but that's normal. Very young children are used to the convenience of the diaper. The big difference between diapers and underpants is that underpants do not absorb the way diapers do, and so when an accident happens, things get uncomfortable. DO NOT go back to a diaper because your child soils her underpants. The exception may be at bedtime.

Instead, do the following: Make the potty as convenient as possible. Place it steps away from your child so that her chances of making it there on time are better. A neighbor of mine actually took the potty outdoors and into their back yard while her child was playing, increasing his chances of making it on time. If your child hasn't used the potty for an hour or two, have her sit down and try. You might run the water, which sometimes helps. Praise and reward your child's efforts and celebrate her success.

> Do not punish if they have an accident, they feel bad enough.

Some children may find it difficult to have bowel movements on the potty. Some children may actually try to withhold a movement rather than go on the potty. This could lead to constipation and other health problems. Consult your doctor if this happens. Your doctor may suggest adding some fiber to the child's diet to make the movements easier. Always encourage and praise. DO NOT punish if your child has accidents; he will feel bad enough. This will happen, so try to take it in stride and be patient. If you are consistent with your support and effort, your child will experience success with this milestone.

V
Eating Habits

Whenever possible, eat meals as a family. Make this a regular, expected routine. Ideally, mealtime should be times to relax and catch up on each other's lives. Encourage all to share something about their day. If nothing is new, ask your children to share something they've learned or something nice they did for someone that day. I learned this from Leo Buscaglia. He was a wonderful author, lecturer, and professor at the University of Southern California. He was referred to as the "love guru" from the 1970s through the 1990s. He died before his time, but his work and words live on. I highly recommend his work.

> Ask your children to share something they learned that day.

One of the stories I distinctly remember him telling was how his very large Catholic family would all sit down to dinner each and every night. His father would insist that they share something they learned that day before they would be excused from the table. He said that he and his siblings were always prepared. They knew what to expect. This was a family ritual and a good one at that. Thanks for the great ideas, Leo.

Require all family members to stay present for a reasonable amount of time. My son, Danny, always came to the table with a huge appetite but with no desire to converse. For one full minute you'd only see the top of his head. When he'd lift his head, his plate would be clean as a whistle. I don't think he even took time to breathe. I would insist he stay for a few minutes and share something about his day. His contribution usually went like this: "School is boring, and recess is fun." I learned to be specific with my questions with Dan, so I could get a response with a little more depth. I would say, for example, "Tell me what you did in science class, and show me a sample of this in your book or homework."

His older sister, on the other hand, loves to talk about anything and everything. When I would ask her how her day was, she would literally begin recounting her day with stepping out of bed in the morning. I would have to interrupt her so that she would eat her meal. I used to tell her to come up for air. She would continue talking even after everyone left the table. She did everything in slow motion. A cattle prod may have been helpful. I jest of course. My youngest, Sydnie, is a good sport about sharing something, but is usually in a hurry to get to the next activity. I have to probe a little with her. I've loved our mealtime conversations, and I am especially proud that my children have all been good eaters.

There should be no phone calls, iPods, texting, TV, or other distractions during this time. The conversation should be light and positive. If you had an especially difficult day at work, try not to ruminate on it. Ask others about the highlights of their day or bring up something that you all are looking forward to. Make sure everyone has a chance to share and that all remain present until this happens. Mealtime is a great time to model good manners, such as:

> Mealtime is a great time to model good manners.

- ✔ Washing hands before eating
- ✔ Helping set the table and cleaning up
- ✔ Chewing with your mouth closed
- ✔ Not talking with food in your mouth
- ✔ Not smacking your lips
- ✔ Asking for food to be passed rather than reaching in front of someone
- ✔ Saying please and thank you

- ✔ Using fingers only for finger food
- ✔ Talking one at a time
- ✔ Keeping elbows off the table

Make the meals nutritious, with lots of variety. Encourage your children to try new things. Most children view whatever is different as bad. As long as you know it's not too spicy or exotic for a child's taste, encourage them to try a little. Mikey did and he liked it! If you're trying something new that didn't quite make the cutting table, there's always the good old standbys: peanut butter, cheese, hot dogs, etc. Finally, don't allow dessert unless your child has eaten a reasonable amount of his meal.

Do NOT make separate meals for family members, except in cases of allergies or illnesses. I once witnessed a neighbor making four meals for a five-member family. I could not believe my eyes. She made a meat dish for her and her husband, a hot dog for her seven-year-old, and pizza for her ten-year-old (with the "gross" cheese pealed off). The children refused to drink anything but juice. The toddler actually ate a variety of finger foods. I joked with my neighbor that she would make a great short-order cook. Her reply was that she couldn't get her family to eat anything else. I responded, "Do not give them a choice. They will get hungry and eat what you've prepared eventually."

This concept is really quite simple. If your children choose not to eat anything that you've prepared, tell them you'll save it for when they're hungry. Wrap it up and put it away. When they ask for a treat—and they will—tell them that they can have one as soon as they eat a reasonable amount of dinner. I've had parents express horror at the thought of their children going to bed without dinner. Not to worry; they will survive the night. They will wake up hungry. Serving them their dinner from the night before may be cruel and unusual punishment. Their breakfast, however, should be something nutritious that you choose. I have a feeling they'll eat it.

I vividly remember an eating incident that occurred when I was three or four. Our family was very poor. How poor were we? We were so poor that my mom was forced to depend on our county food shelf to supplement our groceries. One of the popular items that they generously doled out was cornmeal. We had cornmeal every which way you could imagine, and with every meal. Sometimes it *was* our meal. My mom required that we clean our plates before we left the table. One afternoon I could only manage a few bites of my cornmeal mush. I had had enough. I couldn't take it anymore. I was putting my foot down; I wasn't going to eat another bite as long as I lived.

I sat at that table for what seemed like hours. I was on a cornmeal mush strike. I could hear my siblings playing outside. I begged and pleaded with my mom not to make me eat anymore of the disgusting slop. She ignored me. She simply stood by the sink, did the dishes, and didn't say a word. Then I turned on the waterworks; still not a word from her. She didn't even acknowledge my crocodile tears. What kind of a monster was she?

Then I snapped. I marched up to my mom and bit her so hard on her rear end that my head shook. My mom whirled around without skipping a beat, picked me up, and bit me right back on my derriere. I'm sure it hurt, but I was so stunned that I didn't cry. She then simply pointed upstairs to my bedroom. I ran so fast; I don't think my feet touched the stairs. I did not come back down until the next morning. I don't remember what we had for breakfast, but I know I ate it.

VI
Tantrums

Let's try to define "tantrum." Have you seen *The Exorcist*? Hear about the Tasmanian Devil? A tantrum is an outburst of anger that is often unreasonable or irrational. A child usually throws a tantrum because he hasn't gotten what he wants. But that's just the tip of the iceberg. Underlying issues always precede this behavior. That's a bit of an understatement, but it's true. Tantrums involve a wide range of behaviors, including any of the following: crying, screaming, flailing, kicking, hitting, biting, head banging, spitting, growling, mouth foaming, and breath holding. Yes, I said growling. I've heard it with my own ears, and it's a little frightening.

My oldest child, who eventually became my easiest, is the only one of my children who had a full-blown tantrum. It was only one, but it was a doozie. That day,

Megan woke up at five in the morning and did not go back to sleep. She did not get a nap later on that day because her day care had taken the children on an outing and they didn't get back by nap time. The other children, however, had all napped on the way home in the car. Not Megan.

I picked up her and her brother a little late that day. By the time I arrived, she was ready to blow. We needed to bundle up because it was a cold day. Megan was three and wanted to do everything herself. She struggled to put her jacket on. That's when the tears started. I offered to help her with her zipper, to which she replied, "I want to biz my bizzer." I stepped back, watched, and waited for what seemed like a light year for her to biz her bizzer. I offered to help one more time. That's when she blew. She threw herself on the floor and wailed, but hung on to the bizzer the whole time. I wasn't going to get near that bizzer. While she was down for the count, I thought I'd slip her boots on. Big mistake. She began to kick in her crazed state and caught me on the chin.

That was it; I was done. Her bizzer wasn't bizzed and her boots weren't on. I informed her that she could join her brother, Danny, and me in the car when she was ready. A few minutes later, she walked outside in the snow, unbizzed and bootless. She was livid, and I was taking deep breaths, trying not to lose my cool. I somehow managed to get her in her car seat, but she kicked the back of the front seat all the way home. I glanced in the rear view mirror to see if her head was spinning in a complete rotation.

When we got home, I sent her directly to her room for a time-out. I told her she could come out when she calmed down. After about ten minutes, things got quiet and I checked in on her. She started again. It was a marathon tantrum. Where was she getting the energy? Again, she went back to her time-out. Eventually, she calmed down enough to for me talk to her, though I don't know if she understood anything I said; she was definitely in her own "crazy zone." I was going to let her out for dinner, but she started up again. She was relentless. I brought pizza and milk to her room, set them on her night stand, and left.

I checked again fifteen minutes later. She had eaten half of the pizza; the other half was in her hand and she was sound asleep on the floor. I put her pj's on her and tucked her into bed. The next day I was almost afraid to wake her. But she woke rested and happy and it never happened again.

When you are faced with a tantrum, what should you do?

Let's say that you have determined that your child is having a tantrum because he hasn't gotten something he wanted. So why not just give it to him and end the madness? This will probably work—until he wants something else. By doing this, you have taught your child that, in order to get what he wants, he can simply become the

Tasmanian Devil. This is what you created. When your child is in the middle of a tantrum, the best thing to do is keep her safe:

1. Make sure she cannot hurt herself or others. If you feel that this is a possibility, move her to a safe place and then walk away.

2. Isolate her, if possible, to an area where she won't get attention.

3. If you can't move her, remove any breakable or harmful objects, make sure she is safe, and leave the room. When she realizes that she doesn't have an audience, she'll know that her tantrum is for not. She can't get what she wants if there is no source from which to obtain it.

4. When she's calmed down, a rational discussion is in order.

5. Share and demonstrate how she can use words to express her feelings.

6. A logical consequence should follow this discussion. A time-out in a thinking chair or in another quiet area with no distractions works best. The younger your child is, the shorter this time should be. When it's beyond fifteen or twenty minutes for a preschooler, she may forget why she's

there. When she can show you that she has calmed down and can have a conversation with you, you can end the time-out.

7. After the time-out is over, remind her why the time-out was necessary and what your expectations are. Discuss a better choice to the situation that provoked the tantrum. Again, encourage your child to use words to express herself. Refer to the previous chapter on communication for ideas about good communication methods.

8. Remember to admonish the behavior, not the child.

I recently saw a clip from a video that demonstrated the above to perfection. A toddler was having a full-blown tantrum and was trying desperately to get his mom's attention. When he caught Mom's eye, he would throw himself on the floor and wail. Mom was on the move from room to room. When the toddler looked up and noticed Mom was gone, the waterworks instantly stopped. Each time the toddler caught up with Mom, he would repeat the antics. It was very comical. I'm guessing this went on until he finally wore himself out. The mom was actually doing the right thing. She didn't give him any attention for this behavior, and she didn't lose her cool. She simply ignored him and walked away. The child gained nothing from this behavior, thus discouraging its return.

Do not:

- ✔ Lose your cool; children need good behaviors to model.

- ✔ Yell or scream; two wrongs do not make a right.

- ✔ Give in; children won't respect you, and giving in doesn't help children become independent.

- ✔ Try to reason when they are in the middle of their tirade; it will be ineffective.

- ✔ Show them attention or affection during or after the tantrum; it only encourages and reinforces the bad behavior.

If you are in a public place, try the following:

- ✔ Remove the child to an area where you will not be disturbing others, such as a hallway, restroom, outdoor area, or your car. Return, if possible, when she has calmed down.

- ✔ Don't set kids up for failure and bring them somewhere not suited for children, such as fancy restaurants, long church services, places where you wait in line forever, or places where they have to be still for long periods of time. If you do, you are begging for trouble. Use common sense.

Here's how to prevent a tantrum:

1. Try to reserve some time with your child each day, so he gets the attention he seeks. I realize busy parents can't always do this, but do your best. Get the child involved in what you are doing so you don't have to drop everything. For example, have toys that allow your child to mimic your behavior. When you need to make a phone call, give your child a play phone to use. If you are cooking, let him play with pots and wooden spoons. This way he can spend time with you and you actually accomplish something.

2. Model positive behaviors and communication skills; make sure you and your child use "I" statements.

3. Be clear with your expectations, rewards, and consequences. FOLLOW THROUGH.

4. Make sure children get physical exercise and playtime every day.

5. Monitor the amount of sugar children get.

6. Monitor their play and what TV or movies they watch; avoid violence.

7. Make sure they get enough rest and naps.

8. Make sure they get the amount of nutritious food they need.

9. When in public, always bring the reserves: healthy snacks, drinks, books, favorite toys or stuffed animals, etc.

10. Bottom line, avoid taking the little tikes anywhere if it is nap time or mealtime.

Any tantrum can be an opportune time to teach basic, acceptable communication skills. Please refer back to chapter II for a refresher.

> Avoid taking the little tikes anywhere if it's naptime or mealtime.

You might choose to use a behavior modification program for tantrums if they occur frequently, or for other difficult behaviors. The following outlines a behavior modification program. I've included a sample for reference.

Behavior Modification Program for Tantrums

Purpose: To help children learn positive behaviors by reinforcing and rewarding good choices. Parents should share the desired positive behavior they expect from their child. Discuss how this behavior will be beneficial to everyone involved. Parents should set realistic and reasonable goals.

Goal/Target Behavior: The child will use words to calmly express his feelings. He will accept the decisions that you, his parents, make. The tantrums will occur less frequently and eventually stop.

Plan: Discuss desired communication. Refer to the time the tantrum occurred and the result of the child's choice to have a tantrum. Be specific about where and when the tantrum occurred. Maybe it was at the grocery store when your child did not get the gummy worms he wanted. Remind him of the consequences of his choice. Discuss what would have been a better choice. Role-play with your child. Use puppets or dolls to keep your child's attention, if necessary. Make sure to use the communication skills discussed in chapter II.

> Tell them what to expect if they have a tantrum.

Rewards: Everyone involved should discuss and agree upon these. The reward should be within reason and occur as soon as possible. You can use a behavior modification chart to illustrate the reward system.

Timeline: For young children, the length of time should begin with two weeks. This can be extended if you wish, especially if the outcome is positive. If you've decided to use a behavior modification chart, the child may enjoy having his success posted for everyone to see.

Consequences: Tell your child what to expect if he has a tantrum. Make sure you follow through immediately. Knowing what to expect is a definite deterrent to repeated negative behavior.

How to achieve success:

- ✔ Everyone should discuss and understand the behavior modification program.
- ✔ Everyone should have input and ownership.
- ✔ Be realistic; don't expect too much or too little.
- ✔ Follow through and be consistent.
- ✔ Stay within the agreed upon timeline.
- ✔ Focus on the positive.
- ✔ Reward openly, punish privately.

When should you seek help?

If you and your child have made your best possible efforts, and you've given enough time for his behavior to change but he hasn't responded to your plan, you may need to seek outside help. Rule out any physical problems first with a visit to your child's physician. If the doctor rules out a health problem, an evaluation from a school psychologist or a private psychologist may be appropriate. These professionals will make recommendations that can be very helpful. Please heed their advice and remember, we as parents cannot be expected to have all of the answers.

Behavior Modification Chart

Goal/Target Behavior:

Plan:

Rewards:

Timeline:

Tracking progress can be done using a point system, checks, stars, or smiley faces.

Keep it simple and easy to understand.

Post it where it is visible to your child. If you only mark positive entries on the chart, make it visible for all to see.

Sample:

	SUNDAY	MONDAY
Fell short of Expectation		
Met Expectation		
Exceeds Expectation		

	TUESDAY	WEDNESDAY
Fell short of Expectation		
Met Expectation		
Exceeds Expectation		

PARENTS! GET YOUR HEAD IN THE GAME

	THURSDAY	FRIDAY
Fell short of Expectation		
Met Expectation		
Exceeds Expectation		

	SATURDAY
Fell short of Expectation	
Met Expectation	
Exceeds Expectation	

Point system:

Fell short of expectation = 0 or leave blank
Met expectation = 2 points
Exceeded Expectation = 5 points

Example Rewards:

Daily: One hour your child's choice of play (video game, computer, puzzle, drawing, etc.)

Weekly: Your child's choice of an outing (to the park, a bike trail, a ball game, etc.)

Monthly: New toy (nothing pricey)

VII
Separation Anxiety

This is a common problem that will likely occur at some point in your child's life. Sometimes parents experience this as well. It happens in different forms and to different degrees.

When a child experiences separation anxiety, she feels uncomfortable, anxious, or fearful of being away from a loved one. The anxiety can range from a fleeting thought to a full-blown phobia. The latter is rare, but serious, and sometimes requires professional intervention.

Here's how to keep this kind of anxiety to a minimum:

1. Be honest with children. Let them know when you or they will be leaving. Don't tell them too far in advance or their anxiety may build. If you wait until you're walking out the door, they may panic. Use common sense.

2. Don't dramatize an absence. Be matter of fact and state the facts. Answer any questions children have.

3. Assure them they will be well taken care of.

4. Plan or discuss fun activities they will do with their caretaker.

5. Ask them to be responsible for something while you're gone. For example, have them feed the dog, draw a picture, put a puzzle together, do a chore, etc. Offer a possible reward when you return. This is a great distraction and is good for a child's self-esteem.

6. If they are the ones leaving or being dropped off, allow them to take something from home with them. Having a special object like a little trinket, toy, stuffed animal, or blanket will make them feel connected with home when they are not physically there.

7. Make the good-bye short and sweet. Tell them when you'll return. Don't linger or get caught up in emotions.

When I worked in an elementary school, a mom came to me with concerns about her seven-year-old daughter who was suffering from separation anxiety. The mom dropped off her daughter at a day care every morning before school. And every morning, this entailed drama. In fact, the drama would begin as soon as her daughter woke up. By the time they left the house, her daughter would be crying hysterically. When she arrived at the sitter's house, the sitter would literally peel her daughter off of her. She would go to work an emotional wreck, every day.

I asked the mom to share everything that occurred in the morning before they left. She told me that she would begin to prepare her daughter for the separation as soon as she woke up. She reassured her before leaving that everything would be fine. Often in the car ride, Mom would cry when her daughter cried because she felt guilty about having to drop her at day care. Mom also said that she usually gave her daughter a piece of candy when she arrived at the sitter's house to make the transition easier.

Okay, let's figure out what's wrong with this picture:

- ✔ Mom started her daughter's day by reminding her they would be separated.
- ✔ Mom continued to hammer this home until they were both crying.
- ✔ Mom reinforced the drama by giving the child candy when they arrived.

Mom actually brought on and reinforced the drama herself. The separation anxiety was rooted with Mom, not daughter. Mom inflicted her guilt about working outside of her home on her daughter every day. This needed to stop yesterday. Mom needed to come to terms with working outside of the home and leave her daughter out of it. She needed to put on a happy face in the morning and make mornings as pleasant as possible. As long as work was to be a part of Mom's life, she shouldn't put it in a negative light in her daughter's presence. If she wanted to cry after she dropped her daughter off, that was her choice. Eventually the daughter would view going to the sitters as just a part of life, not a disaster. But getting there would mean no candy and no crying for either of them.

What's interesting about this example is that she was a colleague of mine, a school social worker. She gave great advice to other parents, but when it came to her own parenting, she struggled. The heart and head don't always connect when dealing with your own children.

Many problem behaviors, such as the one just mentioned—or any other covered in this book may improve with the help of a behavior modification program.

Phobias

A phobia is an irrational fear that prevents someone from leading a normal life. This is a deep-seated psychological problem. And phobias can be brought on by allowing or reinforcing a child's fears. Having a phobia can also be a learned behavior, if another family member exhibits the fear in question. Or the phobia could be caused by a genetic tendency or chemical imbalance.

A common phobia for children is school phobia. That is, children sometimes express an irrational fear of school. The reason may be the child's having to separate from her parents or possibly something upsetting at school, anything from a school bully, to a learning difficulty, to a socialization issue. Explore all possibilities thoroughly. Talk to teachers, playground supervisors, and lunchroom supervisors. If your child rides the bus, explore that as a source possible for problems, and make sure to talk to the driver.

The school staff will assist you. Enlist the help of the school counselor, social worker, or school psychologist.

In the meantime, encourage your child to discuss her fears and assure her that everyone is on her side and wants to help. If you explore all angles and come up empty, it might be separation anxiety.

Years ago, I worked with a family that was suddenly experiencing a situation like this with their fourth grader. He had been home with the flu for a few days, and his mom had stayed home from work to care for him. When he was noticeably better (eating well, playing, running, etc.), his mom told him he'd return to school the next day. He suddenly took a turn for the worse. He complained that his belly and head hurt, yet he had an appetite and no fever.

Mom woke him the next day and insisted that he go to school. He began a full-blown meltdown. She couldn't get him to dress or clean up for school. This went on for a week. She called me and we began to explore possible school problems. I spoke with every adult and some students with whom he had contact. I came up with nothing. They all told me that he seemed perfectly happy, got along with others, and did very well academically.

> The heart and head don't always make a connection when it comes to your child.

I asked what happened at home when he stayed home because of his flu. She replied, "The usual; he played video games, went on the computer, and sometimes we played board games." HELLO. Who wouldn't want to stay home with fun and attention like that? That was the big pay-off! She was enabling this behavior. I advised an immediate shift in activities.

I told her, "If you absolutely cannot get him out the door and he claims he's sick, treat the rest of the day as a sick day. He stays in bed: no TV, computer, no games of any kind. He does not get any special meals or snacks. He gets soup; that is good for a sick person. If he does get up and he claims he's better, put him to work. Provide him with a list of chores he will do while he's away from school. Let him know that if he chooses to stay home the next day, the chore list will get longer. He gets absolutely no privileges until he goes back to school. Do not deviate from your plan, or you will be back to square one. The next time he claims to be ill and you're not sure if he's faking, let his physician make the call. Make sure the physician knows what's going on. If everything checks out, stay the course."

If you're in a similar situation and take this advice but still don't get success, what should you do? A mental health evaluation may be in order. Mental health professionals are equipped to assist you with this issue. Follow all suggestions they make, and stick to them. As with any other negative behavior, the longer you allow deep-seated fears to fester, the harder it will be to stop them. Enlisting the entire family to give support during this process will promote success.

VIII
School Performance

You and the entire family should always refer to school very positively. School is a big part of children's lives for many years. Their experiences should enhance their lives socially and emotionally, as well as academically. Attending school is a building block to their future. Your involvement with your child's education will influence your child's learning and enjoyment.

Help your child to get organized. This can be accomplished by making sure to have the tools and supplies she needs. Your child should have an assignment notebook that you can check daily.

Establish a scheduled time each day for your child to do homework, preferably before free time, playtime, TV, or other recreational activities. Teach your child that school is her job and it must come first.

Reward her for her effort and good results. Do not expect perfection, but make sure she is challenged. Show an interest in her school and classes. Get to know her teachers, principal, and other school staff members. Check her school's Web site on a regular basis. Get involved in school activities when your schedule allows. Attend programs that your child is involved in. This will mean the world to her.

If your child struggles in school, consult his teacher and ask for suggestions. The teacher will share how you can assist your child, or she will recommend special help if your child needs it. Be realistic about your child's success.

I once worked with a family with two wonderful boys. They both excelled at different things; one was gifted athletically and the other intellectually. Their father wanted his sons to be more successful than he had been, academically speaking. He had not made academics a priority and, as a result, missed the opportunity to go to college. He was very proud that one son had made great strides academically; we'll call him John. The father often compared John openly to the other son, David. He wanted David to be more like him. He told David, who received average grades, that if he did not make the honor roll, he would not get to play football. David worked very hard and did bring his grades up, but the honor roll was not to be. This started to build a wedge between the son and the father.

SCHOOL PERFORMANCE

The father and mother did not agree on this issue, and it became a problem for them as well. Dad would not let up. He then began ridiculing David and calling him names. He accused him of being lazy and regarded this as the reason for the boy's average grades. This was the beginning of the end for the entire family.

David is now grown, has a career that he enjoys, and is successful in his own right. John went to college and is also doing well. Mom and Dad have since divorced. Dad had dug in his heels and, as a result, completely alienated the rest of the family. He now rarely sees either son. This is an extreme example of what can result if expectations are unrealistic. Regardless of the outcome, we as parents have to be careful to keep our hopes and dreams for our children in check.

> We as parents have to be careful to keep our hopes and dreams for our children in check.

If your child struggles academically, you could try a behavior modification program to address her needs. I discussed this in detail in chapter VI. The following example specifically addresses school performance:

Goal/Target Behavior: To have the child perform academically at average capacity or above.

Plan: This could involve any or all of the following:

- ✔ Input from the child's teacher
- ✔ Tutoring

- ✔ An assignment notebook that you as the parent can check daily
- ✔ A designated homework time each day
- ✔ A homework area conducive to learning, with the least possible distractions
- ✔ Completed homework before the child does other activities

Timeline: The effort should begin immediately. This program should last from two to four weeks. Set partial goals weekly. Check with child's teacher for improvement reports. A very simple chart can show effort, improvement, and your child's reaching the desired goal.

Reward: When your child has completed his homework each day, he can be entitled to a reasonable privilege, such as TV, computer, video game, time with friends, etc. Weekly rewards can include normal privileges, with a few perks. Parents may choose to take away privileges from the start and reinstate them as rewards when they see effort and improvement. When the child has reached his goal, a reward is appropriate. This could be a number of things, such as car privileges for an older child, an article of clothing, or a certificate to a movie theater or movie store. Rewards shouldn't be too expensive.

Consequences: If the child makes no real effort or doesn't achieve positive results, it is appropriate to instate logical consequences. A simple example would be disallowing privileges that evening until your child completes all homework. If your child doesn't meet a weekly goal, withhold special privileges, such as use of the car, her allowance, a later curfew, the phone, or video games. If she hasn't reached the ultimate goal of improved grades within the agreed-upon time frame, stick to the consequences that you've established. Grounding, increased homework time, and extra-credit assignments would be appropriate. When you see improvements, you can reinstate some of your child's normal privileges.

A note about grounding; more than a few weeks of grounding is ineffective.

Resentment builds and the child stops learning the relevant lessons. Instead of deciding on a long period of grounding, have your child earn his freedom back by doing extra class work, research, reading, and doing extra chores.

Extracurricular Activities

Encourage extracurricular activities in your child's interest area. But don't overdo it. DO NOT be one of those parents who insists that their child participate in several activities at one time. Most parents do this for the wrong reasons. Bragging rights somehow make them feel important or superior to other parents. Some parents live vicariously through their children by having them do the things they were unable to. This will backfire.

Children quickly become overwhelmed and stressed out. Other aspects of their lives will suffer, including their social, academic, and sometimes physical health. One or two scheduled activities per week outside of the school day should suffice for elementary-age children. Middle and high school students may be able to handle a few activities, but not if these activities negatively affect other aspects of their lives.

> Activity overload can stress the entire family.

The pressure associated with being overinvolved can lead to bigger, more serious problems. Teens should actually be getting ten hours of sleep per night. This is according to Dr. Alan Green, pediatrician, author of *Raising Baby Greene*, and pediatric expert for Web MD. An adequate amount of sleep for teens is especially important because of the growth and changes teens experience both physically and mentally. They will not get the sleep they need if they are on "overload" with too many activities.

In fact, activity overload can stress the entire family. If you spend too much time being the taxi to all of your kids' events, you'll necessarily neglect other things at home. For example, parents often lose sight of their own needs and relationships with their partner and friends.

SCHOOL PERFORMANCE

It's also important to consider the expense involved in your children's activities. I knew a family that actually went in debt because of the cost of their daughter's activities. Those priorities are wide off the mark. Rule of thumb: family, health, and school must come before outside activities.

Competitive Sports

I have had the privilege of witnessing my children playing sports while they were growing up. These were sports they chose because of their own interests and talents. Generally speaking, their experiences were very positive and taught them a multitude of life lessons, including the following:

> A family actually went into debt to pay for their daughter's activities.

- ✔ Social skills
- ✔ Physical skills
- ✔ Discipline
- ✔ Dedication
- ✔ Sportsmanship

It's been almost twenty years and counting since I've developed "bleacher butt" watching my children. I've witnessed a lot of behaviors during competition, mostly favorable. I have also seen the dark side of sports; the good, the bad, and the ugly. Although mostly exceptions, a few bad apples have stunk up the cart. It just takes one or two bullies to cause a negative ripple effect on the team.

Let's revisit chapter VI on tantrums. Tantrums are outbursts or fits of anger that are often unreasonable and irrational. At sporting events, I have witnessed tantrums and the following behaviors associated with them: yelling, swearing, name calling, spitting, kicking sand, pushing, and threatening. It hasn't been pretty. Sadly, I am not referring to children, but to their PARENTS.

Parents, can you say, "SPORTSMANSHIP"? Come on, parents. It's just a game. No one's life depends on the outcome. The Earth will not open up and swallow you if your child doesn't score the winning run. You are supposed to be the role model, the voice of reason. Parents having tantrums at their children's games is so wrong, in so many ways. Let me count the ways:

> Parents, can you say SPORTSMANSHIP?

1. Children will learn to solve problems with violence.

2. Parents add stress to the entire team.

3. Parents humiliate their children and team.

4. Parents may be "blackballing" their children.

5. Team morale and performance will plummet.

I have my theories about badly behaving parents. They may be unhappy in their own lives and are counting on someone else (namely, their child) to fill a void. They may have unrealistic aspirations that their child will become the next Tiger Woods, Brett Favre, or Jenny Finch. Parents, do you realize these odds are about one in a million? Perhaps such parents have a desperate need to be in control. Maybe they're just not the brightest bulbs in the package. Whatever the case may be, this is absolutely UNACCEPTABLE BEHAVIOR.

As a parent who behaves appropriately (and if you're one, you are in the majority), you may have been a witness to this. Perhaps you've had the misfortune of having a child on the team with the unruly parent. The good news is this: you do have recourse. Unfortunately, you cannot put them in a time-out. Certainly a police intervention is warranted if a parent threatens any physical harm. Expressing your feelings with the coach away from the game is also your prerogative.

If you don't feel your coach is following up on the problem or, worse yet, *is* the problem, contact the league director or board as soon as possible. Depending on the severity of the behavior, the parent may be put on probation or forbidden to attend any more games. This type of behavior should not be permitted to ruin what is meant to be fun and entertaining activities.

I can honestly say that I have had only a three unpleasant experiences with parents and sports. That's not bad for twenty years and counting. Two of these were with coaches with whom I spoke calmly after the game and actually got very reasonable responses. With the third, however, I did not have as much luck. It involved a mom of a girl on a softball team whom I will call "Cruella." It was no secret that Cruella was paddling with only one oar in the water. With her other hand, she must have been holding a wine glass. When booze was added to the mix, things got ugly.

The incident happened at a softball game for my then nine-year-old daughter. Cruella had drunk some wine to relieve the stress of losing the team's first game in a double-header. She felt that one of the girls was not hustling after the ball and thought she might encourage her to try harder by yelling, "Move your goddamn ass!" I couldn't believe my ears. I impulsively said that she could not speak to the girls that way. She then walked away from the bleachers. I discussed this with another parent who wasn't sure what the mom had said. I gave Cruella the benefit of the doubt and apologetically said to her, "I'm sorry, I must have misunderstood you. I thought you swore at one of our girls." Her reply was, "I only did it because she's a lazy ass." With that, I simply walked away.

The other parents and I spoke with the coach after the game. He then told Cruella that her daughter was welcome to participate, but Cruella needed to stay away. Fortunately, she never showed up again. Unfortunately, her daughter had inherited her "gift of gab" and was later removed from the team as well. The "apple doesn't fall far from the tree" theory certainly rang true in this case.

IX
Friendship

Friendship issues are not only possible or probable, they are guaranteed. Why? Because friends matter to children. Children, like everyone, feel the need to be accepted and included. Friends help children develop emotionally and socially. Friends can help kids develop their self-esteem. Next to you, their friends will become the most important people in their lives. In fact, at times your children will value their friends' company, feelings, and opinions more than they value yours. This is a normal part of their development. When children form friendships, they assert their independence.

> Next to you, their friends will be the most important people in their lives.

No matter how old we are, we all remember our best childhood friends, as well as our nemesis. My cousin Joanne was my best friend, and she lived only a few blocks from my family. We saw each other daily, and did what kids do. We had a lot of fun and got into a little mischief. When we were in high school, some of our interests and priorities changed. We still hung out together, but only on occasion. I missed her, but I knew that people change and sometimes grow apart.

After high school, we went our separate ways. We didn't see each other for years, twenty to be exact. We ran into one another at our class reunion. We spent the night catching up, and I was able to tell her how much she meant to me when we were kids. It felt good, because even after all the time that had passed, I had carried those feelings with me. We don't see each other often, but when we do, it's always like going home.

I also remember my nemesis. She was part of what we referred to as the "in crowd." The girls in the in crowd weren't any better than anyone else, but they certainly thought they were. They came from what seemed to be perfect families who lived in perfect homes. They wore perfect clothes, got perfect grades, and had perfect boyfriends. They were arrogant snobs. They looked down on and made fun of others.

They were surrounded by a very small circle of wannabes who did their dirty work. They always had boyfriends because they "put out." I loathed them, but wanted to be one of them more than anything. They seemed to have it all. Life seemed like a breeze to these girls; it wasn't fair. They flaunted their perfect lives, and they didn't deserve it.

My friends and I referred to ourselves as "the outies." It wasn't because we thought we were any less than them, but that we did not want to be viewed in the same light. We used to fantasize about how we would make their lives miserable. But alas, it was all talk and we didn't do a thing. We were taught to do unto others and all that good stuff. They were what are referred to these days as "mean girls," minus the violence.

What's interesting is that, like in the movie *Mean Girls*, they got their comeuppance. By our ten-year class reunion, their husbands had left them and their lives as they knew them had fallen apart. This, however, did not make me happy; it just made me realize that no one's life is perfect.

Mean girls are a modern-day nightmare. These girls do more than gossip and put people down; they get physical. We're talking down and dirty physical attacks. Current statistics show that almost as many teenage girls are being arrested for physical violence as boys. That is a huge departure from just five years ago. Twenty years ago, twenty boys were arrested for assault for every one girl. The ratio today is four to one. Girls in gangs are just as likely to participate in physical altercations as the guys.

The U.S. Department of Justice showed in 1990 that one in fifty criminal juvenile arrests involved girls. By 2003, that statistic grew to an alarming one in three arrests of juvenile girls. The greatest increase was in girls ages thirteen to fifteen.

Why is this happening? There are varying views on the topic. MSNBC asked several teenage girls what their theories were. Here are their responses:

- ✔ TV, media, and the Internet exploit this behavior.

- ✔ Boys egg girls on; they like to watch and post it on the Internet.

- ✔ Girls have been influenced by the reality TV show *Bad Girls Club*.

- ✔ Boys' pack mentality has caught up to girls. In addition, video games portray girls as violent and sexy.

- ✔ Weak family bonding and a lack of supervision allow for a lot of free time and not much parental attention.

- ✔ The girls have no respect for authority.

School officials observe that violence in girls usually starts with foul language, progresses to hand gestures, and then escalate to all-out battles.

What can parents do? The first step is to become aware of this growing trend. Violence is a learned behavior. Consider the following questions:

1. Does arguing and fighting occur commonly in your family?

2. Do you express anger on a regular basis? Does any kind of abuse occur in your home, be it physical, sexual, or emotional? Does the abuse involve alcohol or drugs?

3. Are your children exposed to violence through movies or video games?

4. Are your children often left at home unsupervised?

If you answered yes to any of these questions, your children could be at risk for developing violent tendencies. These behaviors or rituals need to come to a screeching halt. Family counseling is probably in everyone's best interest. Enlist the participation of the entire family. The whole family is affected when any one member, especially a parent, models violent behavior.

If an abuser or violent person refuses help, the rest of the family should pursue assistance regardless of that person. Tackling this problem, especially with teens, won't be easy, but it is doable. Come up with a plan and stick to it, and most importantly, lead by example.

Chances are, the average American family will not have to seek outside help because of violence between friends or family members. Your children will probably deal with the kind of friendship problems most of us did as kids. Because having good friends and being a good friend is so important, your help will be essential. Reflect on some of your own experiences and what you've learned from them. Guide your children through this, and encourage happy, healthy relationships. Children are learning this concept; they have not mastered it. Again, there are a number of variables that affect your child's friendships, some I have already mentioned. Here are a few important influences:

1. What they have learned from the relationships you have modeled

2. Basic behaviors they have learned, such as manners and kindness

3. Their environment, including day care, the neighborhood, their school, etc.

Media Influences

Friendship skills are not innate. They must be modeled and taught. Children need socialization, and it should start at an early age. Parents can begin to expose them to other children when they are toddlers. At that age they will be drawn to other children and show a natural curiosity. Young children of about the same age instantly feel a connection because they are similar in size and exhibit the same behaviors.

> Friendship skills are not innate; they must be modeled and taught.

Children actually begin to make friends around the age of three. If you have more than one child, you have a head start in socializing your child. Day care also puts children in a position to interact. If you are a stay-at-home parent, make sure your child has opportunities to socialize. Plan playdates with friends' children. Check your local library or YMCA for play opportunities for your child.

Toddlers and preschoolers should learn the basics, including the following:

- ✔ Sharing
- ✔ Taking turns
- ✔ Manners
- ✔ Using words to express themselves

These basics should be reinforced throughout their childhood. Parents should observe their children's interactions and intervene when necessary. Note that I did not say rescue. Always give children an opportunity to work things out on their own unless they are involved in a physical altercation.

If your children need help interacting well with other children their age, offer simple suggestions, demonstrate, and have them practice. This can be fun, and can be done with puppets, dolls, or action figures. Recognize and reinforce positive interactions. As they get to be school-age, they can add the following to their friendship repertoire:

- ✔ Using "I" statements and being good listeners

- ✔ Being honest
- ✔ Helping
- ✔ Complimenting
- ✔ Showing interest in others
- ✔ Respecting others
- ✔ Treating others the way you would like to be treated

Regardless of what you practice or teach, your child will experience bumps in the road. Be there for your child when this happens. Be a good listener, and offer simple suggestions. Remind your child that we are human and we all make mistakes. Encourage good communication between him and his friend so they can try to work things out.

If your child is at fault in a disagreement or problem, encourage him to apologize. Role-play if he is open to that. Children should know that they cannot control anyone's behaviors or choices but their own. Have your child examine what he has contributed to the friendship. Has he done his part to maintain and enhance the friendship? Does he have the traits it takes to be a good friend? His coming up short may be affecting his friendships. Suggest a compromise, like it's okay to agree to disagree, and if that does not work, he and his friend may need to take a break or move on to others who are more compatible.

There will be tears; there will be broken hearts. We will feel it with them. Allow and encourage your children to express their feelings. Discourage dwelling on hurts or obsessing. Support your child's choice to move on and occupy his time with healthy relationships and activities.

X
Puberty

Before you read this chapter, I want you to dig into your middle-school-years archives. Find some of your school photos. When you've stopped laughing and can catch your breath, let your mind wander back to those days. Is this too painful or embarrassing? Join the club. They're called the awkward years for a reason. The girls are bigger than the boys. Girls and boys start to notice each other, but don't have a clue what to do.

> Girls get moody and ultra-sensitive, and boys become obnoxious...

Hormones rear their ugly heads. This is the era of zits, body odor, and hair in places it never grew before. Kids' teeth are too big for their heads. They begin to develop groups and cliques. Their self-esteem takes a nosedive. Girls get moody and ultra-sensitive, and boys become obnoxious or silent and isolated. Are we having fun yet?

The good news? This is perfectly normal, and it will pass. The bad news? It isn't easy. What you can expect is the unexpected. So what can parents do?

> Use correct names for body parts, not weiner or hoo-ha.

Start with a huge heap of prevention. Prepare your children for these changes so they aren't terrified when they occur. You must have "the puberty talk" with children by the time they are nine or ten, earlier if they ask questions. Children are developing and changing sooner than we did for some reason. Assuming that they'll get this info from an older sibling or a kid down the block is not a good idea. These are not exactly credible sources. Here are some tips that will help.

- ✔ Use the correct names for body parts, not wiener or hoo-ha (sorry, Oprah).

- ✔ If you are a single parent and your child of the opposite sex is not comfortable discussing this with you, seek out a close family friend or relative who fits the bill.

- ✔ Get your hands on some good, easy-to-read literature to assist you. Good references for girls are these: *The Care and Keeping of You* by Valerie Schaefer and *My Body, Myself for Girls* by Lynda Madaras. A good reference for boys is *My Body, Myself for Boys (What's Happening to My Body)*, also by Lynda Madaras.

✔ Choose a time and place to discuss this where you'll have privacy and no interruptions.

✔ Don't convey any shame or embarrassment, but just that this is part of life.

✔ Make this something to embrace and celebrate. This is the beginning of your child's journey to adulthood.

✔ Encourage discussion. Leave the literature with them for reference.

If you'd like and your children are up for it, make "the talk" a special occasion. With both of my girls, we had a "bra and period" lunch. We went to a local restaurant where I requested a table with a little privacy. I was equipped with some literature, and we just talked. There were lots of yucks and giggles, but it worked. After lunch, we went bra shopping. Boys may not be as enthusiastic about having a one-to-one lunch. I would, however, encourage dads to give it a try, minus the bra shopping, of course.

As an elementary school counselor, I had the duty of presenting the human growth and development (aka puberty) information to the fourth-grade girls. The parents were invited to join their children, and many of them did. I suggested the "bra and period" lunch. Many of them took me up on this suggestion and reported back to me how much fun they had. That your child will experience puberty is a fact of life that is inevitable, so why not enjoy it?

Having information on hand will help them to feel prepared when these changes occur. Girls should be equipped with bras and feminine napkins even before they need them. Boys and girls should both have deodorant and acne products. Being prepared and knowing what to expect will help them immensely in getting through those awkward years.

Parents, be patient with your children and try not to overreact during this time in their lives. Try to be understanding and maintain a sense of humor.

XI
Peer Pressure

Peers are people of the same age, sometimes friends, who have similar interests and experiences. As children become independent, their peers play bigger roles in their lives. At some point, your kids may be spending more time with their peers than with their family. In fact, throughout life they will continue to gravitate toward peers, especially those peers who have similar values and interests. This is normal. They feel comfortable with this group, and they can relate to and empathize with them.

Peer pressure is the felt need and desire to fit in with this group. Peer pressure can be good, especially when children are influenced to join a team or club that can enhance their lives. A peer may have a hobby or activity that will peak your child's curiosity and could broaden her horizons.

Sometimes, though, the desire to fit in, be accepted, and liked can cause stress. Children may find themselves compromising their principles in order to belong. This can become a problem. Peer pressure comes in different forms, external and internal. The external pressure is not just from friends but can also be from media, movies, magazines, etc. Internal pressure occurs when a child lacks self-confidence or is insecure, and his or her need to become someone else is intensified.

> Children may find themselves compromising their principles in order to belong.

Sometimes kids get skewed ideas of what they should be and who their peers are or should be. The media in particular presents a range of ideals, many of them inappropriate, and kids respond. Peers may be portrayed as beautiful and talented, or in other words as perfect. This, of course, isn't reality, and perfection is impossible to live up to. But kids will feel that they have to try, and puberty is a time when the pressure to try is especially influential.

Teens with loving, supportive families and who have good self-concepts usually don't get totally sucked in by this. Others who may not have this support or may be going through a rough patch could fall prey to this façade. If you think your child is buying into this notion, by all means intervene. Discuss the problem of perfection, for example. Nobody is perfect. Everybody is good at something, but no one is good at everything. Remind your child of all the wonderful qualities she has, and encourage her to make the most of it. Celebrate differences and encourage your child to do the same. Steer your child toward positive relationships and activities.

Discuss healthy ways to cope with stress. Good stress-busters include talking with someone the child trusts, journaling, and exercising.

If your child feels pressure from friends to be someone she isn't, discuss good decision making. Ask your child the following questions:

- ✔ Can we weigh the pros and cons of what you are considering? Let's consider the consequences and determine if what's required is worth it.

- ✔ What is at stake? Could saying yes jeopardize your safety, get you in trouble with the law, with us your parents, or with your school?

- ✔ Might you lose your true friends in the process of trying to be like others?

Let children know they can come to you anytime about anything. Be a good listener, and don't freak out. That will promote regular dialogue with them. Children who are secure and content with family relationships are less likely to become dependent on peer approval. Children who lack loving, healthy relationships with their family are more dependent on, sometimes desperate for, peer connectedness.

Suddenly some older, seemingly cool kid comes along offering glamour, drugs, and protection.

The word "gang" comes to mind. The pressure to join a gang may be the most dangerous form of peer pressure. Older, savvy, street-smart thugs prey on younger, vulnerable, lost souls. According to statistics from the National Youth and Gang Center, these vulnerable kids are often boys who do not have fathers present in their lives. They may be in a situation where a single mom is preoccupied with trying to make ends meet. They grow up feeling insignificant and develop low self-esteem. They need to feel like they belong somewhere, but don't have the tools to express their feelings or the guidance to make good choices.

These are frequently the same kids who get bullied. Suddenly some older, seemingly cool kid comes around and offers them glamour, drugs, and protection. That's a no brainer; drugs to make them forget what a loser they are and no more getting their butts kicked by the bullies. What more can you ask for?

This honeymoon, however, is short lived. Gang initiation often involves physical violence. The enlistee either gets a beating or is forced to do dirty work by violating someone else or breaking the law. Once a kid joins up, the gang owns him; good luck getting out. If parents find their child in a situation like this, police intervention is best. They will advise you and your child about the best way to get out, and stay out, safely.

XII
Sex

This three-letter word is the one that most parents dread. The thought of your little darling "doing it" is almost unfathomable. Try not to visualize. That is especially painful. It's almost as painful as them visualizing their parents. Yikes! The day your child has sex for the first time will come; it's a fact of life. It's a normal, healthy act, when a person is ready for it. When is someone ready? When they are at least thirty and have been married for five years. (Okay, so that's the parent in me speaking.) Ideally, young people should wait until they are consenting adults, but things don't always work out that way. Many teens have sex before they are emotionally and intellectually ready for it. The repercussions

> The thought of your little darling "doing it" is almost unfathomable.

of this are endless.

There are many things parents can do to help children make responsible decisions regarding this very serious subject. Hopefully you had "the talk" when they were going through puberty. When they are teens, it's time to get down to the brass tacks. Again, choose a time and place that are conducive to a private conversation. I always found that talking while driving in the car worked well. In that context, there aren't too many other options besides conversing.

Wherever you choose, not having to make eye contact with you sometimes puts kids at ease. Share the facts and remind them of the "how things work." Try to keep the conversation low-key and informative. Let them know that it is normal to be curious and experience certain feelings and desires. It is healthy to discuss and educate them on the topic. The more they know, the better.

Teens are less likely to take sexual risks if they know what the consequences can be. It is also your responsibility to fill in the blanks if they miss something. I recently watched a sitcom that dealt with this topic. A teenaged girl came home with a hickey on her neck. The parents were concerned that what led to the hickey could lead to more intimate sexual activity. In a very funny sketch, the parents showed their daughter very vividly colored diagrams of different sexually transmitted diseases (STDs). It was a hilarious scene, and it actually had a lot of merit. Theirs was not a bad idea; those STDs were all possible consequences.

Kids should know the other very critical risks, including the following:

- ✔ Pregnancy
- ✔ AIDS or other sexually transmitted diseases (STDs)
- ✔ Psychological problems
- ✔ Relationship problems

They are all worth discussing, but pregnancy and AIDS deserve delving in to. These two outcomes will dramatically affect the rest of their lives. We'll begin with pregnancy. All teens should be required to spend endless hours around infants and toddlers. This could be the best birth control possible. When my youngest was born, my older children were thirteen and fifteen. The timing was perfect. I couldn't have asked for more, with the endless crying, pooping, and spitting up. It was awesome. My teens were scared straight.

> All teens should be required to spend endless hours around infants and toddlers.

Unfortunately most teens do not always have this opportunity, nor would they want it if they did. Hit them where it hurts. Share the following outcomes of having a baby too soon:

1. While their friends are partying, they'll be babysitting.

2. They will have to put college on hold so they can work full time at a job or two they don't like to support their child for whom they will be financially responsible until that child turns eighteen.

3. They may feel pressure to get married when they're not ready, or be a single parent, which is one of the most difficult jobs on Earth.

4. They can say good-bye to a full night's sleep, watching movies or ball games without interruptions, mall shopping, skate boarding, gambling, clubbing, unlimited texting, video game marathons, spring break, going out to eat, doing anything on a whim, etc., etc., etc. Need I go on?

If you happen to know someone who has experienced a teenage pregnancy, share that example. Better yet, if you know someone in that situation or who has been there, ask him or her to share. This is usually more effective, especially if the story comes from someone close to their age to whom they can relate.

I was fortunate as a teenager to witness my sisters' misfortunes firsthand. When I was sixteen, my two 17-year-old twin sisters became pregnant within three months of each other. To say it was a disaster is an understatement. My mom was in shock for months. I remember a lot of crying over two events that, under different circumstances, would have been celebrated. It was an eye-opener for me. I'm convinced it was the most poignant, effective lesson I could have learned about birth control. There was no sexual activity for this girl for quite some time.

My sisters were seniors in high school. They not only were forced out of the extracurricular activities they were involved in, but also were forced out of school. They were required to stay out of sight and go to night school. They missed out on all the fun senior activities their classmates were doing including senior prom, senior banquet, senior skip day, and senior retreat, not to mention all the parties around graduation. When their classmates went to the all-night party the evening of graduation, they stayed home with morning sickness and heartburn.

The worst was yet to come. The parents involved forced them to get married. They might have been in love (or lust), but neither my sisters nor their boyfriends were ready for marriage. They all had big plans. One sister was an honor student on the college track. The other sister, the creative one, wanted to pursue an art career. Neither plan came to fruition. The honor student moved into a small dormlike apartment with her new husband. He was a college football player. When he wasn't playing or practicing football, he was out with his buddies. My sister was home alone in a small apartment caring for her infant daughter in a city where she knew no one. She cried and complained a lot to her new husband and then the abuse started. She wasn't aware at the time that he was cheating on her. After several years of abuse, she got the courage to leave. They eventually divorced.

My other sister's story isn't quite as bad. She, however, was unable to pursue her dreams and her husband was forced to drop out of college to get a job he didn't like. They lived in a small trailer. They were both stuck in dead-end jobs and resented each other for it. Infidelity plagued the marriage and eventually they divorced. They suffered and their children suffered.

Their lives scared and saddened me. Their misfortune was a life lesson for me. Teens need to hear these stories, so that they don't have the romantic views of baby, family, and happily ever after. Having a baby can be the best gift of your life, WHEN YOU'RE READY.

Pregnancy does offer other options, including adoption or possibly abortion. These choices are also tremendously difficult and can have serious ramifications. No matter what the decision, it will be difficult and it will stay with your child for the rest of her life. A huge dose of prevention is always best. Again, educate your children; be real and offer them literature. Whether you expect that your child may or may not have sex, do discuss birth control. Make sure kids know what their options are, where to get them, how they work, and how effective they are. If your children are in steady relationships, regular reminders are a good idea. Abstinence is always the most foolproof method, but educate them about all of their options and be realistic.

The interest around AIDS has seemed to quiet down. However, according to the Department of Health and Human Services, Centers for Disease Control, it is still among us and still very dangerous. Prevention is always a wise idea. It is important to keep in mind that AIDS can be contracted through heterosexual sex. It can also be spread by drug users sharing needles. Babies can become infected by a mom who has AIDS/HIV. It is not exclusive to sex between males, as was once believed by the general population. If a sex partner is a carrier, it can be contracted through oral, anal, or vaginal sex. In the United States, females make up 26 percent of those contracting HIV. Worldwide statistics show that there are more HIV cases among women than men. This is most likely due to males having multiple female partners and, unfortunately, because many women are raped by men infected with this disease.

The reprecussions of AIDS and pregnancy are unlimited.

Contracting other STDs is also possible when a person practices unsafe sex. The herpes virus and genital warts, for example, are not curable and require ongoing treatment. Genital lice (or crabs) can spread from one person to the next, even with a condom. Gonorrhea and syphilis are also contagious diseases and can be very dangerous if left untreated for any length of time. Contrary to popular belief, STDs can also be contracted through oral sex. Some teens don't even refer to this as sex.

It's always a good idea that any person and that person's partner be tested before having sex if either has had different sexual partners. The best protection again is abstinence, but sexually active couples should use condoms until thorough testing proves them both disease free. Again, speak frankly with your teens and offer them good literature for reference. I highly recommend the following Internet resources:

- ✔ The Palo Alto Medical Foundation's "Teens and Sex: Information for Parents": www.pamf.org/parents/sex/teensex.html

- ✔ Plannedparenthood.org's "Teen Talk": www.plannedparenthood.org/teen-talk

- ✔ Sex, Etc.: www.sexetc.org

- ✔ Avert.com's "Teens' Pages": www.avert.org/teens.htm

Although sex is a physical act, like it or not, a lot of emotions are involved. These emotions can range from euphoria to guilt and regret. Sex is a big deal, and it needs to be treated as such. If your teen is not sure about having sex when facing the opportunity, that should be her first red flag. If your teen feels pressured in any way, that's another red flag. Some guys still use that tired old line, "If you loved me you'd have sex with me." Oh, please; are you kidding me? I sure hope our young girls are too smart to fall for something that lame. Hopefully that would be enough to stop them in their tracks. If not, they will experience a boatload of anxiety that will last a long time after the sex act. Remember: it's not just sex. It's an act that will define a very important chapter in a young person's life.

A bad reputation is certainly not life threatening, but it can make the teen years very painful.

"If you loved me, you'd have sex with me."

Whenever young people put themselves out there and take risks that they may regret later, there's a chance they'll get outed. This is especially true if the teen has casual sex with more than one partner. Even in today's society, when teen sex doesn't shock like it used to, frequent casual sex still hits a sour note. I hate to say this, but this is especially so with girls. As preposterous as it is, boys are often revered by other boys for having many sex partners or conquests. Yes, we've come a long way baby, but with many issues, the playing field is still not equal. It's sad but true. A teen shouldn't count on even her best friend keeping secrets; sooner or later, secrets about sex leak. With today's technology, texting, Facebook and MySpace, word travels fast. This can be devastating, and there are no do-overs. The emotional upheaval will pass, but your child will not forget.

Just recently a mom shared her tragic story regarding her daughter's "sexting" suicide on the *Today Show*. I saw it, and as a mom, it made me shutter. Losing a child is the worst pain a parent can experience. When that child takes her own life, the parents feel especially lost.

The woman's daughter had texted a naked picture of herself to her then-boyfriend. After they broke up, the ex-boyfriend forwarded the photo to many other teens. The ridicule from others was relentless. This left her miserable and depressed.

She put on a brave face for a while and seemed to cope. She then had a set back after attending a friend's funeral. Later that day, her mother found her hanging in her bedroom.

We all make mistakes, especially as teens. Teen brains aren't fully developed, and so young adults tend to make impulsive decisions. Teens tend to do things on whims, without much forethought. This does not make them bad people. This does not mean they are incapable of making good, sound choices, but they sometimes need to illicit help from a caring adult. They can learn from their mistakes and move on to healthier lifestyles. A supportive adult can guide teens down better roads and help them avoid repeating the things that did not work for them. Doing things differently takes some reflection and a lot of trial and error. Teens have a whole lot of life ahead of them. There is plenty of time to right a wrong. Encourage them not to dwell on the past, and get them the help they need to move forward.

Sexual Orientation

According to the American Academy of Pediatrics, "sexual orientation originates mostly from the biology that people are born with. A person's psychology and environment may also influence sexual orientation." They further state that "no one can cause or prevent one's orientation."

Many gay and lesbian teens feel judged by their peers, society, and even sometimes their own families. Coming out for some, especially for teens, is difficult and painful. As a counselor specializing in chemical health, I've had many referrals who were gay and lesbian teens. They struggled with their sexuality because it was socially unacceptable. Some of them had come out, but were being bullied on a regular basis. In some cases, they chose to hide it and live a lie because of the fear of repercussions.

> In one extreme case, a sixteen-year-old was disowned by his family when he "came out."

In a few cases, the parents became cold and distant after their teens came out. In one extreme case, the parents of a sixteen-year-old boy disowned him when he came out. He became a runaway and spent most of his time in a homeless shelter or on the streets. All of the students I happened to see self-medicated to numb the pain they experienced; most of them became addicts.

111

These cases, as sad as they are, pale in comparison to what happened to Matthew Shepard. Shortly after midnight on October 7, 1998, twenty-one-year-old Matthew Shepard met two men at a bar. The men singled him out because he was gay. They offered Shepard a ride in their car, which he accepted. Later, in a deserted, remote, rural place, Shepard was robbed, pistol whipped, tortured, tied to a fence, and left to die. A passerby discovered him eighteen hours later. Shepard was alive but in a coma.

His injuries were too severe for doctors to operate. He never regained consciousness. He died on October 12, 1998. Although this is an extreme act, unfortunately violence against gays and lesbians is not isolated. Hundreds, perhaps thousands, of crimes have been committed against gay and lesbian people because of their sexuality.

On March 20, 2007, the U.S. Congress met to consider the Matthew Shepard Act. The intent was to extend federal hate crime legislation to include gay, lesbian, and disabled people. The bill passed in the House of Representatives, but President Bush vetoed it later that year. President Obama has stated that he is committed to passing the act.

I am very happy to say that times are changing. There are still people who choose not to understand what it means to be gay and lesbian in contemporary culture, but not as many actually say or do anything hurtful. We have a very active GLBT (gay, lesbian, bisexual, and transvestite) group at the school at which I work. This is attended by gay and straight alike. Many of these students are school leaders and role models.

We are also very fortunate that most of our society is beginning to view gay and lesbian people differently than they did years ago. We still have a ways to go, however. As people are willing to learn more about sexual orientation, they are realizing that this is not a choice, but a part of who people are. It is in fact just a small part of the total package, just as heterosexuality is. Homosexuality does not define gay and lesbian people. Have you ever heard someone point out a person that he or she thought was gay? I have, many times. Have you ever heard someone say, "Hey, check out that guy; I bet he's heterosexual?" Neither have I. If we don't think that being straight is a defining piece of what makes a person human, why should we think being gay or lesbian is?

Parents, I urge you to support and embrace your children for who they are. Sometimes, our children may not be what we expected, but this doesn't make your children wrong. Encourage them to be the best that they can be, whatever that is. To help support your children, a good Internet resource for parents and teens is www.advocatesforyouth.org/glbt.htm.

XIII
Drugs

Drugs is another topic of conversation that can begin when children are toddlers. Keep it simple. Let them know that there are good drugs and bad drugs, and that most drugs can help you feel better but some can make you very sick. Too much of even a good thing can be very bad for you. Putting a Mr. Yuck sticker on medicine bottles speaks volumes. This is something they can relate to. You can place this sticker on any household product that is harmful. Your best bet is to simply keep such things out of reach and locked up if necessary.

This is not a time to shelter your children or be in denial about what's happening in our society.

As children get older, they will hear and see things that reference mood-altering drugs, some legal some illegal. This is not a time to shelter your children or be in denial about what's happening in our society. Having honest, open discussions is always a good idea. When children reach elementary age, there is no need to delve into all of the intricacies of illicit drugs. Share what you know but keep in mind their capacity to understand.

Alcohol is still the most used and abused drug in the United States. If you drink alcohol, drink in moderation. If you teach your kids that drinking is a bad thing for them to do but you do not drink responsibly, you send the wrong message. Remember, parents are their children's role models, and even if they don't like what you are doing, they learn from what you do. Too much alcohol can lead to addiction and many other health, legal, social, and emotional problems.

When someone in the family is addicted to alcohol, it affects everyone. Even if the drinker tries to hide it, alcoholism's effects rear their ugly heads in many ways. The characteristics of a problem drinker can range from a tendency to isolate to moodiness to raging. It can lead to different forms of abuse, abandonment, divorce, or loss of employment. It can also cause liver disease, heart disease, an ineffective immune system, and many different forms of cancer. It can lead to illegal activities, violence, drunk driving, and death.

Make sure your children know that alcohol is a drug. This drug causes more deaths each year than all illicit drugs combined. The *Journal of the American Medical*

Association estimates that a total of 85,000 deaths per year are alcohol related. The estimated number of deaths from all other drugs combined is 17,000.

When I was in college, the drinking age was eighteen. This was not a good thing. Most students didn't just use alcohol, they abused alcohol. I know; I was one of them. But I just drank, I didn't use drugs; I thought that it was no big deal. That was my attitude in college until one beautiful Saturday afternoon at a football game. Football season was awesome. The games were the highlight of my week. I knew several players on the team. It was my sophomore year. I had a year of drinking experience under my belt. I was already an old pro. I believe I had a few beers before the game that day. Alcohol was not allowed in the stadium, but many students snuck it in. I'm sure that's no big shock to anyone. One of the traditions at the games was to pass a bottle down the row. The person who finished the bottle dropped it under the bleachers; it would smash and everyone in that area would cheer.

This took place all over the stands. That day it took place just a few rows in front of me. Students passed the bottle down the row and one of the girls skipped the drink and passed it on. She got all kinds of grief for doing this. The bottle got passed back to her as her friends chanted "Go, go, go . . ." She chugged what looked like a half of a fifth of something brown (whiskey, brandy, or tequila). She dropped the bottle; it smashed and

117

everyone cheered. Mind you, this girl weighed maybe a hundred pounds soaking wet. I could not believe she was able to do that; I was a beer girl myself.

After a few minutes, she passed out. Her friends got a big charge out of that. But then the tide turned. They could not wake her. I could see them patting her face and saying her name. One of them picked her up and carried her down the stands. This drew a lot of attention, and people didn't know what to think. A police officer offered his assistance, but quickly realized he needed help. EMS was already at the game and promptly arrived to assist. An ambulance whisked her away. The mood at the game became very somber. People stayed, but the crowd was hushed.

The next day I saw a friend of mine who was a campus police officer. I asked if he knew anything about the girl who was taken by ambulance from the football game. He said, "Yes, I'm familiar with that case." I had to pry it out of him, but finally he said, "She died from alcohol poisoning." I felt like I got the wind knocked out of me. "Alcohol what?" was my response. I didn't know you could die from drinking alcohol. I was so naïve. I had come from a long line of heavy Irish drinkers. I had witnessed much more alcohol consumption, and it had never caused a death. I'd seen people pass out, lose their lunch, and a do lot of other nasty things, but death? Not in my wildest dreams.

That was my wake-up call. I still partied and I did imbibe, but on a much smaller scale. The visual of that young woman being carried down the bleachers and placed in the ambulance is still as fresh in my mind today as it was thirty-five years ago. I now share this story with my students and my own children. Binge drinking is a growing problem with teens and at colleges throughout the country. Warn your children of the consequences of drinking alcohol. Advise them not to participate and if a friend does, by no means should they just let that friend sleep it off. He or she may not wake up. If your child finds himself in a situation in which he cannot rouse a friend by shaking, or if the friend's breathing is very shallow, your child should get that person medical attention at once.

As parents, our responsibility is to educate our children about all of the dangers involved with drinking. When they are old enough and in moderation, they can choose to drink. Or not. I hope your children learn this by living it, because you are great teachers and role models. Talk to them and listen. As their questions get tougher, you can reference reliable resources. One that I highly recommend is www.theantidrug.com.

Marijuana

Marijuana use is a close second to alcohol nationwide. It has surpassed alcohol use by teens. More teens today are addicted to and seek treatment for marijuana dependency than any other drug. This may surprise you, but it's not "just marijuana" anymore. Today's marijuana contains ten times more THC than it did when I was a teen. THC is the main chemical in marijuana that makes you high. Back in the 1960s, 1970s, and 1980s, it was less harmful. The THC levels were between 2 and 5 percent. They are now between 20 and 25 percent. Some of the marijuana imported from Canada and Mexico is up to 50 percent THC, which makes it a hallucinogenic and highly toxic.

Today's marijuana has more cancer-causing ingredients than do cigarettes. If you use both cigarettes and MJ, the chance of getting cancer is forty times more likely than someone who does neither. Marijuana, unlike most other drugs, stores in your white blood cells. Long after the high wears off, the MJ stays in your system. If you are a moderate user (who uses once a week), MJ will stay in your system up to two weeks. If you are a regular user (who uses two to three times a week), it will stay with you for about a month. If you are a chronic user (who uses regularly for six months or more), MJ can stay in your system for years.

> More teens are addicted to marijuana than any other drug.

There are so many things wrong with marijuana. Lets start with brainpower, which is dramatically decreased under the influence. Your brain is made up of mostly white blood cells. When they are jammed with MJ, they do not work well. As we now know, even when the high wears off, the marijuana is still with you, hence the effect on concentration and short-term memory. The brains of people between the ages of fifteen and twenty-five, the ages when a person's brain is going through a huge growth spurt, are especially sensitive to mind-altering drugs. Regular use of MJ during this time can actually lower a person's IQ.

A student once told me after he finished treatment for MJ addiction that he didn't feel dumb anymore. He could actually focus in class and remember things. The moral of his story? Marijuana wreaks havoc on a person's short-term memory.

Speaking of white blood cells, when they are full of MJ, they do not do what they were intended to do, namely fight off viruses. A regular user will be much more susceptible to upper respiratory diseases. Males who smoke MJ for a long period of time may also be rendered impotent. So guys, if you think that children may be in your future, even your remote future, you might want to lay off the weed.

Oh, and that high that users search for? They have it for a few minutes, then they come down and feel worse than before. This is a bummer dude, but it's true. When MJ enters the brain, it releases a feel-good chemical called dopamine, which gives the high. But soon after the brain is left with a shortage of that chemical; that's why users feel worse after they smoke than they did before they smoked.

Regular use of MJ can completely deplete the brain of dopamine, leaving users depressed. In fact, they no longer experience the high from MJ, but just experience a kind of a blah feeling. That's why they call it the "gateway" drug—because users eventually move on to chase a different high from something stronger.

I'm sorry if I perseverated about marijuana, but too many people have the misconception that it's harmless. Once I was working with a student who had recently left treatment. She had been using many different drugs, and treatment for her was imperative. However, after a few months, she relapsed and was returning to her using ways. Her parents were at a loss and came to me for advice. I recommended they immediately get her back into aftercare, including counseling, meetings, and having a sponsor. I also helped them develop a behavior modification program for her and drew up a contract that would help them all stay on track.

A few days later, my student stopped in and was happy to report she was doing great. I said, "I am so pleased you're clean." She said, "Yeah, I am, except for weed." I said, "Well, then that's not clean." She told me that her parents were willing to compromise on her contract as long as she was just using weed. I could not believe what I had heard. JUST WEED? I thought that she had to be kidding. Her father confirmed this news with me. People like these parents and this kid need to understand how different today's weed is from that of years gone by. It's not "just weed" anymore.

So what can parents do to prevent drug and alcohol use? I've already mentioned a few important components: communication and positive role modeling. There are many other strategies that help. The following is a review and addition to what I've already shared. These strategies can help with all behavior problems, but others less serious don't always require this much attention.

1. Be involved in your child's life. Attend and show interest in her activities and hobbies. Check with her school on a regular basis to see how she's doing. Schedule regular family times, meals, games, recreation, etc. Get to know your child's friends and her friends' parents.

> Once they have betrayed your trust, they have lost their right to privacy.

2. Set limits. Be clear about rules and expectations. Be consistent and follow through. Punishments should fit the crimes. Acknowledge and reward good behaviors. Above all, be a good role model.

3. Communicate. Talk and listen. Use "I" statements. Pay attention to your child's body language. Don't argue. Sometimes you might have to agree to disagree or take a break in the discussion.

4. Reassure your child that she can come to you with any problem. Note sudden

changes in her behaviors, moods, eating or sleeping habits, friends, grades, or attendance.

5. **Do not:** overreact if they confide or confess that they have used; allow them to drink alcohol at home; leave them unsupervised overnight; allow friends to leave and return to a get together at your home.

6. If you have reason to believe your child is using and have found evidence, such as empty liquor bottles or drug paraphernalia, randomly search her, her room, and her belongings. Once she has betrayed your trust, she has lost her right to privacy and she should have to earn it back. Random drug tests are also in order at this time. If your child refuses, treat this as an admission of guilt. A consequence is in order. Hit them where it hurts: limit or suspend her cell phone use. This is likely what she uses to make drug connections. Limit or suspend the use of the car. Refuse sleepovers (that's where a lot of the trouble brews). Tighten up curfews. Confer with your child's friends and their friends' parents.

Signs of Drug or Alcohol Use or Abuse

Physical signs that your child is under the influence include the following:

- ✔ Eyes that are bloodshot; pupils that are dilated or constricted.
- ✔ Speech that is slurred, delayed, or very fast.
- ✔ A gait that is unsteady or unusual.
- ✔ Actions that are goofy, hyper, or in slow motion.
- ✔ An unusual pungent or skunky odor; this can be from alcohol or marijuana.

Behavior may be or involve the following:

- ✔ Secretive or isolating
- ✔ Defiant or defensive
- ✔ Moody
- ✔ Lying/stealing/selling their things
- ✔ Poor attitude
- ✔ Lack of motivation
- ✔ Paranoia

Friendships can sometimes indicate trouble. Look out for the following:

- ✔ Changes in friends
- ✔ Older friends
- ✔ Refusal to bring friends home to meet you
- ✔ Loss of friends

Changes in activities such as the following can indicate use or abuse:

- ✔ Quitting activities they once enjoyed
- ✔ Decreased skill or performance in activities

School performance may change as follows:

- ✔ Poor attendance or tardiness
- ✔ Late or missing assignments
- ✔ Falling grades
- ✔ Inattentive or sleeping in class
- ✔ Behavior problems

Your child's health may also suffer in the following ways:

- ✔ Sudden weight loss or gain
- ✔ Fatigue
- ✔ Hyperactivity or nervousness

- ✔ Ongoing upper-respiratory problems
- ✔ Deterioration of hygiene or appearance

Parents, if it looks like a duck, walks like a duck, quacks like a duck, it's a FREAKING DUCK!

The key is to look for behaviors that are very unlike your child's usual behaviors. I implore you to get involved if your child shows the above signs. They are not normal, nor are they a phase. Don't ignore them or accept excuses from your child. This is NOT the time to stick your head in the sand. If your child won't fess up, then start doing some digging and investigating. Search his room, check his cell phone, give random drug tests, and check up on him. If you come up empty, bring him to a physician for a thorough exam.

> If it looks like a duck, walks like a duck, quacks like a duck, it's a FREAKING DUCK!

I have made these suggestions to several parents I have worked with, and about 50 percent of those parents have followed up. They usually find that their child is in fact using. About half of this group then does something.

I remember distinctly two very serious, separate incidents in which the parents did nothing. Both sets of parents were insulted by my suggestion that their children might be using. Both sets of parents complained to my supervisor that I was too pushy.

In the first example, a sixteen-year-old boy I'll call "Joe" began to change drastically. His grades plummeted;

he skipped school and was moody and disobedient at home. He was, however, showing up, out and about with new clothes, cell phone, watch, and iPod. He told his parents that he made these purchases with money he had made mowing lawns the previous summer. They didn't question it. When rumors started to float around school that he was dealing, I shared this with the parents. They refused to believe it or to search his room or car. That, they said, would be an invasion of his privacy.

Three months later, the police followed up on a tip and searched their house. They found a large amount of marijuana, scales, and baggies. They also found over $1,000 in cash. He was charged with intent to sell, which is a felony. He spent the remainder of his high school career in juvenile detention.

The second example is more tragic. I'll call this boy "Tom." He was a senior in high school. He ranked academically in the top 10 percent of his class and was a gifted athlete. He was headed for an ivy league university the following year. He was also unfortunately a drug addict. His parents knew that he drank beer and smoked weed on occasion, but didn't think he had a "problem." He arrived at school one day already under the influence of something. His first-hour teacher sent him to the office, and I also met with him. His eyes were red and glassy, and his speech was slurred. His gait was unsteady, and he had a difficult time holding up his head. He said that he had the flu and had taken some cold tablets.

He gave his mom the same story when she arrived to take him home. I told her that I wasn't buying it, and suggested she take him to the ER for testing. She was insulted by this and admonished my behavior. Less than two months later, he overdosed on methamphetamine. He survived, but was in a coma for months. He has permanent physical and neurological damage. His prognosis is dismal. He will probably never exceed the aptitude of an eight-year-old.

Please, parents, step up to the plate. Your children's lives depend on it.

If you have established use:

- ✔ Assess the severity of the situation. Is it isolated or ongoing?
- ✔ Take your child to your physician for a drug test.
- ✔ Discuss the severity of the situation with your child.
- ✔ Give your child a serious consequence for using.

If the problem is ongoing or the situation is life-threatening:

- ✔ Have a chemical health assessment done (check your insurance to see if your policy covers this).

- ✔ Follow up with recommendations.
- ✔ If your child becomes combative or threatening, contact the police.

I know this all sounds scary. The good news is you may never have to deal with serious drug issues. If you do, I guarantee these strategies will help. Remember, if parenting is not hard work, you are not doing your job.

If you are supporting your child's sobriety, this could be a good time to use a contract, along with the other interventions mentioned. A contract clearly states your child's goals. Give your child the support and incentive she needs to stick to the contract. All parties involved should discuss and agree on the contact's terms. Date it and include a time frame in which your child should expect to reach her goal. All parties must sign this document to show that everyone is involved.

Revisit the contract regularly to check on progress. This is a great time to praise and reward positive behaviors. If your child has broken the contract, you may need to tweak it slightly. A consequence would be appropriate, or you may need to add an intervention to get your child back on track. Remember: the consequence should fit the crime, and more importantly, you're all in this together.

The following page is a sample of a very basic behavior contract.

BEHAVIOR CONTRACT

Name: _____

Date: _____

Desired behavior:	
REWARD for desired behavior:	
Privileges to be reinstated:	
Additional rewards:	
Consequence for breaking contract:	
Privileges suspended:	
Additional consequences:	
Timeline:	

Signatures:

Mother:	
Father:	
Child:	
Witness: (if desired)	

XIV
Internet Safety

Each day, Americans are becoming dependent, obsessed, or even addicted to computers, video games, and cell phones. The vast majority of our homes have computers and video games. Adults and teens commonly have cell phones. There is no question that their use is beneficial in countless ways: communication, information, and entertainment, to name a few. These are all great tools to have at our disposal. But the old adage that we can have too much of a good thing rings through loud and clear when it comes to these items.

The Internet seems to be the biggest culprit. How much of the Internet is too much? If using the computer prevents you or your child from leading a normal life, you or your child may be bordering on obsession or even addiction. If some or all of the following are negatively affected by a person's Internet use, that person is in trouble:

- ✔ Decrease in work or school attendance and or performance
- ✔ Neglected relationships
- ✔ Interrupted sleep
- ✔ Deteriorating health
- ✔ Making Internet use the priority in life

MySpace and Facebook have become wildly popular among youth and adults. They are social networking tools that connect people with friends and others who work, study, and live either around them or across the globe. Connecting with others in this way is a healthy and enjoyable way to pass the time, in moderation of course. A privacy setting can be used to deny access to both Facebook and MySpace sites. This is a good safety feature, but it can also prevent parents from entering their own children's sites. When children know their parents won't see their information, they tend to push the limits. They may share too much personal information, which puts them at risk for exploitation, sexual predators, and other general dangers.

> When children know their parents won't see their information, they tend to push the limits.

One of the major disadvantages of the Internet is

its lack of supervised content. For this reason, it is possible for our children to be enticed into using alcohol or drugs by what they encounter online. Web sites that they access can also contain bizarre and dangerous instructions, such as how to kill yourself or others and how to make explosives. Granted, your average teen will disregard these sites. But a slightly disturbed teen who may be teetering between reality and fantasy could be influenced.

Parents need to become computer savvy. I have to admit, my ten-year-old is probably more computer savvy than I. I'm still learning; I have a longer curve. Parents should find out what sites their children visit and talk with their children about what's appropriate.

Limit children's time using the computer, playing video games, and using their cell phones. Children also need to spend time moving and exercising. Remember exercise? Surfing the Internet does not burn a whole lot of calories. And at any rate, homework and studying should come first. Using the computer can be a privilege kids earn after they complete their schoolwork. Find a common place for the computer where all family members can access it. Parents can block the content and online chat rooms they feel are not well suited for their children.

A federal law, the Children's Online Privacy Protection Act (COPPA), was created to help protect kids online. It's designed to keep anyone from obtaining a child's personal information without a parent knowing about it and agreeing to it first.

COPPA requires a Web site to explain its privacy policies on the site and get parental consent before collecting or using a child's personal information. The law also prohibits a site from requiring a child to provide more personal information than necessary to play a game or participate in a contest.

COPPA offers the following advice to parents to insure a child's safety on the Internet:

- ✔ Share an e-mail account with children to monitor messages.

- ✔ Bookmark kids' favorite sights for easy access.

- ✔ Monitor your credit card and phone bills for unfamiliar charges.

- ✔ Find out what online protection is offered at your children's school or anywhere they can use a computer without your supervision.

- ✔ Follow up on any complaints from your child about an uncomfortable online exchange. Share this with your Internet provider.

- ✔ Forward copies of obscene or threatening messages to your child to your Internet service and the police.

INTERNET SAFETY

✔ Contact the police or FBI if your child has received any transmission of child pornography.

✔ Never allow your children to exchange any photographs over the Internet or in the mail.

✔ If your child has a new "friend" online, insist on being introduced.

✔ For more information, check out this Web site: www.connectsafely.org.

> Contact the police or FBI if your child has received child pornography.

XV
No Do-Overs

Parents have the good fortune to have their children under their wings during the most important part of their lives. You shape and mold your children for their futures, their adulthoods. You will influence their behaviors, personalities, interests, values, and habits. You only have one shot at this, so make it your best. If you screw up (and you will), no worries. Step into those chaps, pull up your bootstraps, get back on that horse, and ride. Oh, what a ride it will be.

> Step into those chaps, pull up your bootstraps, get back on that horse, and ride.

There will be ups and downs and twists and turns that you never imagined. It reminds me of a movie I recently watched for the umpteenth time, *Parenthood*, which I highly recommend.

The senile grandma makes an analogy about parenting. She compares it to a roller coaster ride, with all the ups, the downs, the twists, and the turns. She says that she could have chosen the easy path and gone for a ride on the merry-go-round. That is, she could not have had children. Merry-go-rounds only go around and around. They are predictable and boring.

Instead, she chose the roller coaster (in fact, she had four children), which was exciting, scary, exhilarating, and unpredictable. It made life more interesting, meaningful, and worthwhile. If she could do it again, she would definitely choose the roller coaster. As that grandma knew, having children is the epitome of life's sweet ambiguity. Every day is an adventure.

But there are no do-overs. Your children are with you for eighteen or so years. It may seem like a long time if your children are young, but trust me, it goes by in a flash. Having two adult children, I look back and wonder where those years went. I picture my little curly-haired girl making snow angels when she was five or six and how beautiful she looked for her junior prom. I can see vividly my toe-headed boy running on the playground in elementary school and kicking a fifty-yard field goal in high school. Now they are both college graduates.

These memories always bring tears to my eyes. I cannot go there too often or I'd be a blubbering mess. I was fortunate enough to have my youngest child—my little whoops when I was forty-four, but already I see her growing too fast and a day closer to leaving the roost. I still refer to her as my baby and she's ten. My mom still calls me Babe. I didn't like it when I was a kid, but now it has a nice ring to it.

Our time with our children is a mere pittance compared to the big picture. This is our big chance to pay it forward. We parents can begin an important ripple effect with our children. By touching their lives with love and careful attention, they can touch and influence so many others. Our children will emulate our kind words and gestures and pass them on to others. By being great parents, we can positively affect our community, society, and beyond. Sounds far-fetched? It actually makes perfect sense. We are in a position to make a difference in countless lives. Why not go for broke? Think about that the next time you offer to help your children or they witness you doing a good deed.

> This is our big chance to pay it forward.

People often ask me which stage of my children's lives was my favorite, and I say the one that they are in right now. It just gets better every year. I see them blossoming every day and growing into their own incredible personae.

I can definitely pick out some of the most memorable moments of my time as a parent. When my oldest, Megan, was six, her father and I were going through a divorce. It was an incredibly painful time for all of us. I felt responsible because I had initiated the divorce. The pain and guilt I felt at the time were overwhelming. Children are very intuitive, and my Megan knew I was hurting, even though I spared her the details.

I of course was more worried about the effect the divorce would have on my children than anything else. One morning at work, I reached into my briefcase to get something and I found a beautiful handwritten note from Megan. She had written six words that I'll never forget: "I luv yu no matr wat." My little angel had made the note in her very best handwriting and slipped it into my briefcase. It was a turning point for me. It gave me the strength to move forward and made me realize that the love between a parent and child is unconditional. I still have that note in my briefcase. I pull it out every once in a while as a reminder of what a blessing she is. It definitely puts things in perspective when I'm having a bad day.

My youngest, Sydnie, is incredibly caring and helpful. Recently my mother became very ill. She had a debilitating stroke. It was a full day before she was discovered and by that time it had progressed to a very serious stage. This left her paralyzed on her left side, unable to speak, and with partial brain damage. She spent a few weeks in a hospital then had to be moved to a nursing home for physical therapy. Her physical therapy was very difficult because she was experiencing a great deal of pain. Further medical tests revealed that her cancer, which had been in remission, had returned and metastasized to her bones. The prognosis was very dismal. I was completely distraught.

When I heard the news about the cancer, I went to my room and sobbed. Sydnie came in and sat down next to me. She didn't say a word. She put her arm around me with her head on my shoulder and stroked my back. I honestly don't know how long she sat with me, but when we sat down it was light out. At some point, Sydnie asked if we should turn a light on and I realized it had gotten dark. That brought me back to reality. I was done feeling sorry for myself and was now focused on how lucky I was to have such a thoughtful little girl.

I've saved mentioning my son for last. It's not because this memory is the best, but it certainly involves the most unexpected event. No, Megan and Sydnie, this does not make him my favorite.

My two girls have always been very outgoing and gregarious. Dan, on the other hand, is the strong silent type. I swear that kid didn't utter a word until he was three. In fact, when he was very little, I was a little concerned, until one day I realized that his sister was doing all of the talking for him. When she was not quick to respond, Dan would look to her for an answer, as if to say, "Hey, sis; get with the program. Answer already." We finally put the kibosh to this and he was speaking in full sentences in no time. He never did inherit his sister's gift of gab; he simply wasn't interested. When he had something important to say, he said it; otherwise, he didn't waste his breath. As he got older, I got an occasional, "I'm fine" or maybe a grunt. Any parent-child PDAs (public displays of affection) stopped when he was about ten. When we did see each other in public, I barely got eye contact. But I digress . . .

Dan was the kicker on his football team in high school all four years, and all four years he was voted MVP. Twelve years of soccer had given him quite a boot. He made all-state two years in a row and was recruited to play big ten football. But the highlight of his career came at the end of his junior year in high school. His team was playing its conference rivals, and each team was vying for first place. The other team took a quick lead and even though we played catch up, we found ourselves down two points down with three seconds on the clock. Our team was on the opponent's thirty-eight yard line. The coach decided to have Dan's team—and that meant Dan—kick a field goal. That meant a forty-eight-yard kick. It wasn't his longest kick, that had been a fifty-three yarder, but he was now under real pressure.

There he was, waiting for what seemed like an eternity to kick that freaking ball. The whole kit and caboodle was riding on his shoulders. He readied to kick twice and the opponents called two time outs. When he finally kicked it, he nailed it! They won the game and the conference title. The crowd went crazy, and teammates lifted him up on their shoulders. But this is far from the best part of the story.

I waited with the crowd after the game as I always did, to give him an "atta boy." That is, if I could get close enough to him. There were at least five hundred people waiting that night. The team finally emerged from the locker room; again, a roar from the crowd. Dan was in the middle of the pack. When the crowd spied him, they began to chant his name. It was surreal, but this still is not the best part. Dan worked his way through the crowd, nodding in appreciation and smiling. He continued to work his way through the crowd, in my direction.

A group of cute cheerleaders was in front of me, and I was sure he was headed for them. But as he forged ahead, he looked like he was aiming for me. I turned around to see if someone was behind me, but there was no one. He stopped when he reached me, put his arms around me, placed his head on my shoulder and cried, in front of God and everyone. I felt as though I was having an out-of-body experience. After a few minutes he said, "Mom, this is the best moment of my life." I thought a few seconds and said, "Dan, your wanting to share it with me makes it the best moment of *my* life."

That was a once-in-a-lifetime moment. Lightning could've struck me dead after that moment and it would have been okay. I felt complete. Okay, I'll say it: "They complete me." Sorry, I couldn't resist. It just simply doesn't get any better than that. These incredible moments with my children trump all the poopie diapers, screaming fits, sassy mouths, and nights when they stayed out past curfew. Granted, the examples I've shared were not everyday occurrences, but I'll take what I can get.

Studies show that children don't truly appreciate their parents until they are twenty-three. I have my theories about this. Maybe it's the age when they are given their walking papers and they are truly on their own. It's not so easy out there in that big bad world. That time didn't fully come for me until I was twenty-eight, when my first child was born. I had read all the books, checked what the experts and the not-so experts had to say. I was ready; this was going to be a new venture, but not a difficult one. I was pumped and prepped. When Megan came along, I was singing a different tune. What was that famous Beatles song? Oh yeah, "HELP"!

That's when I realized how truly amazing my mom was. She was a single mother of four by the age of twenty-one. She had very little help from her family because they disapproved of her divorce. My biological dad was out of the picture early on. He decided shortly after I was born that he couldn't handle the responsibility of four children. My mother received no child support or support of any kind from him. She needed to make weekly trips to the county office food shelf to supplement our groceries. Just the thought of cornmeal mush still makes me cringe. But she did the best she could with what she had, and she did it with flare. Those were the good old days—NOT.

She was very loving but also tough as nails. She didn't put up with any BS. I'll never forget an incident that happened when I was in the eighth grade. I had snuck into a high school dance with a partner in crime. My mom somehow caught wind of this. I swear she had a sixth sense. She showed up at the dance. I didn't notice at first, because I was staring at the hunky guy dancing next to me. I finally got his attention and even a little smile, then his attention shifted and his expression changed. His eyes got big and he stopped dancing, as did the others around me. Then someone gently but firmly grabbed my arm.

I'd have known that hand anywhere. Much to my horror, it was my mom. I was so embarrassed I wanted to die. When I looked at my mom however, embarrassment was quickly replaced by fear. Kids snickered as I sheepishly left the dance with my mom. Not a word was said on that fifteen-minute (but what seemed like hours-long) ride home. When we got home she was too angry to give me my punishment. I went straight to bed. She said very little the next day; words weren't necessary.

I didn't see the light of day for two weeks. I finally worked up the courage to ask how long my sentence was. She said that if I wanted to leave the house, I'd have to work my way out. The following week consisted of my doing every possible dirty job our house had to offer: picking up dog poop, scrubbing the toilet, and cleaning the oven—and back in the late 1960s, there were no self-cleaners. I didn't complain, but I was pretty pathetic. After a week of being Cinderella, my mom cut me loose. Trust me, I didn't pull that stunt again.

She wasn't just the ruler of the roost. She was always there for all of us. She chaperoned most of our high school dances. She was the chauffeur for our gang 95 percent of the time. Everyone congregated at our house. She was definitely the "cool" mom, yet she commanded respect from everyone. She didn't miss an activity of ours unless she was deathly ill. I was a basketball and football cheerleader in high school. She attended every sporting event I cheered at, all four years, except for one game; she had bronchitis. I didn't think much of this at first, but found myself looking for her in the stands. Her not being there left me feeling a little empty inside. She was my own cheerleader, my mentor, my confidant, and my mom. Not too many people can say that about a parent. How fortunate I was. I didn't tell her this until I had my own children. I then realized the sacrifices she had made for us.

> How the hell did she do that and remain sane?

I'm thankful to her for teaching me invaluable life lessons. When I had children, she instantly became my hero. How the hell did she do that and remain sane? She endured poverty while raising four children on her own. She somehow survived living with an abusive alcoholic husband. She held her head high and supported her pregnant teenage daughters while the town gossips had a field day. While my brother was in Vietnam, she managed a brave face that disguised her constant anxiety.

It has been thirty-five years since we've all left, and she still says those were the best years of her life. I sometimes whine about how difficult being a parent is, then I think of her and I bite my tongue. I was much older when I had children; I had a steady income and the father of my children around to help. The thought of her quickly snaps me out of my pity parties. She has inspired me to make the best out of a difficult situation.

I thank God every day, and I'm not a religious person. My life is richer because I've been blessed with a great teacher and three awesome kids. Because of them, I am more giving, kinder, more patient, and definitely happier. I'm stealing your line, Jack; "They make me want to be a better person."

> They make me want to be a better person.

Index

A

abuse, 17–20, 85, 105–6, 126–27
academics, 15, 65–67, 69–75, 84, 126
accomplishments, 6
active listening, 14–15
addictions, 116, 122–24, 133
AIDS, 103, 107
alcohol, 18, 116–19, 125–27
American Academy of Pediatrics, 111
anger, 12–13
anxiety, 61–65
apologies, 23, 88
appreciation, 146
arguments, 20
arrests, 83–84
Avert, 108

B

babies, 29–30
bad dreams, 33–36
bedtime routines, 34–35
behaviors
    alcohol abuse and, 125, 127
    consequences of, 16, 52, 57, 73, 102
    contracts for, 9, 130–31
    enabling, 63, 66–67
    lack of rules and, 7–10
    modification programs for, 56–60, 70–73
    for potty training readiness, 39–40
    tantrums and, 49
    See also specific behaviors
belittling, 20
best friends, 81–82
binge drinking, 119
birth control, 103–7
blackballing, 76
bonds of parent/child, 1–2
boundaries, 5–10, 12
bra and period lunch, 93–94
brainstorming, 25–26
bullies, 76, 98
Buscaglia, Leo, 43–44

151

C

charts, behavior modification program, 59–60
chemical imbalance, 24
child pornography, 137
children
    communication and, 24–25
    comparisons of, 21
    dreams for future of, 70–71
    expectations and, 5
    friends of, 23
    parent bonding and, 1–2
Children's Online Privacy Protection Act (COPPA), 135–37
communication
    basics of, 24–25
    conversations, 44–45, 115–16
    of fears, 66
    importance of, 7–9
    mealtime and, 44–45
    peer pressure and, 97
    principles for, 26–27
    questions and, 14
comparisons, 21
competition and sports, 75–79
complaining, 31–32
compromises, 15, 88
computers, 133
conferences, teachers, 70
consequences, 16, 52, 57, 73, 102
contracts, 9, 130–31
COPPA (Children's Online Privacy Protection Act), 135–37
corporal punishments, 21
counseling, 85
credibility, 12
criminals, 83–84
criticism, 14

D

deaths and alcohol, 116–17
decision making, 97
Department of Health and Human Services, U.S., 107
Department of Justice, U.S., 83–84
depression, 7–10
disagreements, 88–89
disappointment, 6
discipline
    grounding, 73, 147–48
    potty training and, 41
    spankings, 21–22
    techniques for, 12–14, 16, 50–53
divorce, 141–42
Donnelly, Denise, 21
dopamine, 121
dreams, 33–36, 70–71
drugs
    alcohol, 18, 116–19, 125–27
    case scenario, 127–29
    conversations about, 115–16
    interventions for, 129–30
    lack of rules and, 7–10
    marijuana, 119–22
dry run, 38
dysfunction, 17–20

E

education, 15, 65–67, 69–75, 84, 126
emotions, 1–2, 24–25, 61, 108–9
    See also specific emotions
enabling, 63, 66–67
expectations, 5
extracurricular activities, 73–75

INDEX

F
Facebook, 134
family counseling, 85
family meals, 43–45
   See also mealtimes
fears, 65–66
feedings, 30
feelings, 1–2, 24–25, 61, 108–9
   See also specific emotions
friendships, 23, 81–89, 95, 126

G
gangs, 98–99
gateway drugs, 119–22
gays, 111–13
girls, 83–84
Green, Alan, 74
grounding, 73, 147–48

H
health and alcohol abuse, 126–27
HIV, 103, 107
homework, 15, 69, 72–73
homosexuals, 111–13
hormones, 24, 91
hypocrites, 16–17

I
"I" statements, 26, 27, 55, 87, 123
Ianelli, Vincent, 35
illicit drugs, 116
independence, 6
infants, 29–30
influences, 86–87
Internet, 133–37
interventions, 129–30

J
Journal of the American Medical Association, The, 116–17
juvenile delinquents, 83–84

L
Larzelene, Dr., 22
lesbians, 111–13
lifestyles, 2–4
listening, 14–15
love, 6

M
Madaras, Lynda, 92
manipulation, 31
manners, 45–46
marijuana, 119–22
Mayo Clinic Foundation for Medical Care and Research, 32
mealtimes, 30, 39, 43–48
Mean Girls, 83
media, 35, 36, 86–87
memories, 140–45
mental health issues, 24
mentors, 16–17, 19, 23
mistakes, 15–16, 23, 110
mood altering drugs, 115–16
   See also drugs
Mr. Yuck, 115
MSNBC, 84
MySpace, 134

N
name calling, 20
National Youth and Gang Center, 98
neglect, 17–20, 85, 105–6
nemesis, 82–83
newborns, 29–30
nightmares, 33–36
"no," 6

153

O

obsessions, 116, 122–24, 133
open-ended questions, 14
opinions, 15, 88
overinvolvement in extracurricular activities, 73–75

P

pacifiers, 31–33
Palo Alto Medical Foundation, 108
Parenthood, 139–40
parenting, 1, 4–5
parents
    child bonding and, 1–2
    concerns, 11–12
    dreams for children's future, 70–71
    drug interventions, 129–30
    emotions, 1–2
    expectations, 5
    memories, 140–45
    as role models, 16–17, 23
    rules for, 10
    single, 146–49
    tantrums by, 76–79
    united fronts and, 12
Pavlov's theory, 31, 38
peer pressure, 95, 97–99
perfection, 96–97
phobias, 65–66
physical problems, 24
picky eaters, 46–47
Planned Parenthood, 108
police, 83–84
pornography, 137
potty, 41
potty training, 37–40
pregnancy, 103–7

preschoolers, 87
pressure, 73–75, 96–97
profanity, 20
puberty, 91–94
punishments
    discipline techniques, 12–14, 16, 50–53
    grounding, 73, 147–48
    potty training and, 41
    spankings, 21–22

Q

questions, 14

R

reflecting, 15–16
relationships, 1–2, 85
reprimanding, 13–14
reputations, 109
resenting, 73
respect, 22
rewards, 39, 56–60, 70, 72
ridiculing, 20
role models, 16–17, 19, 23
role-playing, 16, 57, 88
routines, 15, 34–35
rules, 5, 7–10, 12

S

Schaefer, Valerie, 92
schools, 15, 65–67, 69–75, 84, 126
screaming, 21
security, 6
self-esteem, 6, 62, 81, 91, 98
self-reliance, 6
separation anxiety, 61–65
Sex, Etc., 108
sexual behaviors, 93–94, 102–9, 111–13

INDEX

Shepard, Matthew, 112
siblings, 21
single parents, 146–49
sleep, 29, 33–36, 49–51, 74
social networking, 134
socialization, 86–87
spankings, 21–22
sports, 75–79
STDs, 107
Straus, Murray, 21
stress, 73–75, 96–97
support, 96–97

T

tantrums
    behavior modification programs for, 56–60
    behaviors and, 49
    by parents, 76–79
    prevention of, 55–56
    in public places, 54
    sleep and, 49–51
    tips for, 51–53, 54
teachable moments, 15–16
teacher conferences, 70
technology, 26–27, 133–37
teenagers, 74, 83–84, 102
television, 35, 36
    See also media
text messages, 109–10
THC (Tetrahydrocannabinol), 119–20
"the talk," 93–94, 102
threats, 12
thumb sucking, 32
time-out, 13, 51–53
toddlers, 24–25, 37, 53, 87

U

underwear, 40
U.S. Department of Health and Human Services, 107
U.S. Department of Justice, 83–84

V

violence, 84

W

whining, 31–32

Y

yelling, 21

155